VEGAN VITALITY

Captivating Cuisine for a High-energy Lifestyle

Vegan
VITALITY

Captivating Cuisine for a High Energy Lifestyle

DIANE HILL

Illustrated by Juliet Breese

*Food Preparation, Styling and
colour photography by
Paul Turner and Sue Pressley,
Stonecastle Graphics, Maidstone.*

THORSONS PUBLISHING GROUP
Wellingborough, Northamptonshire

Rochester, Vermont

First published 1987

© Diane Hill 1987

British Library Cataloguing in Publication Data

Hill, Diane
vegan vitality : captivating cuisine for a high-energy lifestyle.
1. Vegetarian cookery
I. Title
641.5′636   TX837

ISBN 0-7225-1341-0

Printed and bound in Great Britain by
Hazell Watson & Viney Limited,
Member of the BPCC Group,
Aylesbury, Bucks

CONTENTS

		Page
	Introduction	7
1.	The Nature of Veganism	21
2.	The Vegan Dairy	29
3.	Soups	41
4.	Pâtés and Starters	49
5.	Main Courses:	
	Tofu dishes	59
	Pulse dishes	66
	Nut dishes	73
	Seed and grain dishes	85
	Pasta, pancakes and pastry dishes	94
6.	Salads	108
7.	Sauces and Dressings	123
8.	Vegetables	134
9.	Puddings and Desserts	142
10.	Cakes and Biscuits	156
11.	Breads and Quickbreads	167
12.	Instructions for Making Soya Milk and Tofu	179
13.	Kitchen Tips and Information	182
	Index	189

INTRODUCTION

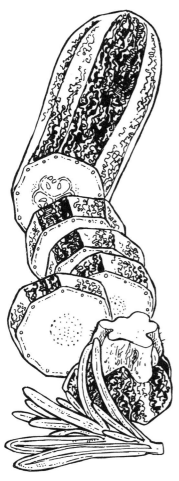

We live in an age in which people are placing increasing emphasis on the *quality* of life. No longer are we naively impressed by claims that something is the biggest or fastest thing on earth. Now we want to know if it is *worth while* and if it will enhance the *value* of our lives. The rapid growth of interest in fitness, health and diet since the 1970s is symptomatic of this changed outlook. While once we ate the mass-produced and processed food that benefited bulk producers, greedy manufacturers and anonymous supermarkets, now we are beginning to demand food that is to *our* benefit. We want food that is healthy and which does not contribute to diseases and bodily malfunctions. We want it to be ecologically sound, and not to cause undue suffering to animals. In short, we want food that adds to our enjoyment of a full, varied, healthy and caring life.

It began with vegetarianism. Now, with ever-growing support from nutritionists, dieticians and recognized food experts, veganism seems to be the correct and natural solution to healthy and compassionate eating in the late 1980s. Veganism is taking off in a big way and, like vegetarianism, it has left behind prejudices about crankiness.

This book does not set out to convert the entire population, nor does it preach veganism in a 'holier than thou' tone. What it does intend, though, is to present an informative but easy-to-understand introduction to veganism, both as a way of eating and as a way of life. I hope that this will dispel any misconceptions that it is frugal, monotonous or extremist.

If you are not used to vegetarian, let alone vegan, eating, the vegan collection of culinary ingredients may seem restricted at first. Vegetarians, as most people know, do not eat meat or fish. Vegans go further than this and exclude foods derived indirectly from animals, such as milk and eggs. People who have not tried veganism tend to assess it in negative terms: no meat, no fish, no eggs, no dairy produce, and usually no honey — what on earth is left? And so it may seem to anyone who has been brought up on a staple diet of meat and two veg.

When you begin to explore the wealth of vegan alternatives to conventional dishes, however, you soon discover a fascinating and highly appetizing array of flavours, textures and combinations that satisfy every possible taste-bud! There are delicious milks, creams, butters, and cheeses, colourful and tasty savoury dishes based on staples such as pulses, tofu, nuts, seeds, grains and cereals, and tantalizing vegan versions of creamy desserts, cakes, ice-creams and confections. Only in the vegan household, for example, would you find such a choice of easily-made or commercially-available milks to pour over your breakfast cereal, or creams to enhance your strawberry pie.

But let us consider the main arguments for adopting, or at least leaning towards, a vegan diet. In the first place, it is very healthy.

The health and fitness aspect

In recent years there has been a major rethink about nutrition throughout the Western World. Independent research has developed an international consensus. This is no flash-in-the-pan set of opinions which will change in a year

or two, like the specialist strands of 'research' which proclaim the short-term wonders of a grapefruit diet or that eating mounds of fat will leave you sylph-like in X weeks. Several decades of research have led to widespread agreement between public, governmental, scientific and medical bodies, all over the world. Experts and distinguished bodies such as the World Health Organization (WHO), the Royal College of Physicians, the Committee on Medical Aspects of Food Policy (COMA) and the National Advisory Committee on Nutrition Education (NACNE) have striven to establish some positive proposals for future food policies.

There are many reasons why substantial changes in the average Westerner's diet are felt to be necessary. One only needs to look at the statistics related to the 'Western diseases of affluence' (that is, conditions which are rare or unknown in Third World countries). These include disorders and cancers of the digestive tract, diabetes, and diseases of the heart, circulatory and vascular system, and there has been an alarming and consistent rise in their incidence since the Second World War. In the UK, which now has the highest rate of coronary heart disease in the world, having recently overtaken Finland and the USA, cardiovascular disease alone is responsible for over 50 per cent of the deaths of men between the ages of forty-five and fifty-four, while the various cancers account for another 26 per cent of deaths in this group.[1]

Diet and disease

What has all this to do with diet and nutrition? Studies conducted worldwide over many years have concluded that diet and disease, particularly the 'Western diseases', are crucially related. Furthermore, it is the 'average, typical diet'[2] of the West that is the culprit. 'In short, we are all of us at risk' points out Colin Tudge in his excellent book based on the NACNE report (the

NACNE report was published by the Health Education Council in September, 1983) and related research documents. Although he has no vegan axe to grind, Tudge points out that there is a significant exception to high blood cholesterol and its associated illnesses amongst 'lifelong vegans'.

Tudge safeguards his argument by referring only to 'lifelong' vegans, because of some evidence that cholesterol-related diseases such as atheroma (a condition which involves crystallization of cholesterol in the arteries) might not be reversed once established. I would, however, point out two important facts, for the sake of non-lifelong vegans like myself as well as for those wishing to improve their health by changing the emphasis of their diet. First, research has consistently shown that reducing intake of saturated fat and cholesterol *does* significantly reduce blood-cholesterol levels within a comparatively short time (experiments conducted in Italy and Finland, for instance, showed a drop of approximately 20 per cent within as little as six weeks).[3] Second, that these reductions do seem to lessen the incidence of disease.

Because of their high incidence of heart disease, the governments of the USA and Finland have urged people to follow the nutritional guidelines set out by NACNE. As a result, there has been a notable decline in the hold of the major Western diseases. In the USA, for example, cases of fatal coronary heart disease fell by 3.6 per cent per year between 1968–1977,[4] and are continuing to decrease as people's awareness of the importance of healthy eating and living increases.

The NACNE report argues strongly for major and immediate dietary reform, stating in its preface that its intention is to propose a programme for the 1980s which will be relevant, feasible and worth while for the population as a whole. It stresses the need for an encompassing public health policy as opposed to any more 'selective' approach, which would offer little hope of appreciably reducing the national incidence of disease in the UK.

Over the last couple of years alone the media coverage of the relationship between diet and disease has increased dramatically. Television programmes have underlined the Health Education message, while a number of radio programmes have increased the public's knowledge of diet and health. Newspaper and magazine articles have also introduced readers to healthy alternative eating patterns.

Food production methods

So we can see that earlier ideas about diet were inaccurate and had to be revised. But that is not the whole story. Modern, high-technology production methods in farms, factories and factory-farms have increased the risks to health by treating the consumers' 'choices' of food with substances and processes which can have a toxic effect on the body. Debate about the need for more stringent legislative controls on the intensive farming of animals, for example, has arisen largely because of the high incidence of stomach cancer which occurs in intensive farm workers.[5] This suggests a possible link between the effects of such methods on the product and the development of serious physical abnormalities in the consumer. There is also the question about the inhumane conditions and treatment suffered by the animals, a subject to which I will return later.

This may all sound unduly alarmist, but if one follows the debates and research, and listens to the chief protagonists in the health/nutrition lobby, one can well understand the note of urgency in their call for positive changes in eating habits and food production policies.

Recommended dietary changes

What then do these proposed changes amount to? We have talked in general terms about the *need* for dietary reform. Now it would be helpful to home in on the particular reforms which are advocated. The basic recommendations of NACNE are as follows:

1   To cut down on our consumption of fat, which presently provides, on average, over 40 per cent of the total energy in the British diet, to about 30 per cent of our daily intake of energy in food.

2   To keep down our consumption of saturated fat (which is derived chiefly from animals and animal products) to not more than one-third of that 30 per cent limit of total fat, so that it provides no more than 10 per cent of the daily energy intake.

3   To reduce the intake of sugar (this includes brown sugars and substances like honey and golden syrups) by 50 per cent, which would bring consumption down from current levels of 40 kilogrammes (88 pounds) or more, to about 20 kilogrammes (44 pounds) per head per year. Further, not more than half of this reduced amount should come from snack foods like sweets and confections.

4   Fibre intake should be increased by about a third to about 30 grammes (1.2 ounces) per day, and this should be derived chiefly from a greater consumption of wholegrains and whole-cereals.

5   Salt in the diet should be reduced by about 25 per cent to not more than 9 grammes ($\frac{1}{3}$ ounce) per head per day.

The eating of more unrefined foods would also, the report suggests, help to control weight because whole foods from plant sources are less calorie-dense and are more filling than more refined foods or animal products. They therefore provide energy without 'overloading' the system with calories.

How much protein?

The report does not contain any recommendations about protein, because it is felt that too much unnecessary and possibly damaging emphasis has been placed on protein in the past. Since the Second World War right up to the 1970s, we have been told by authorities such as the Ministry of Health that we must eat plenty of protein. If we did this, it was declared, all other needs would generally follow in its wake. The most concentrated forms of protein were to be found in animal flesh and animal products, so the increased production of these foodstuffs was actively encouraged. Many people still believe that meat, eggs and dairy produce are the core of a healthy diet. However, we are now beginning to realize that these foods are high in substances like cholesterol and saturated fat.

What is more, research has shown that we do not *need* the large or concentrated inputs of protein obtained from animal sources. Our bodies function much more smoothly and efficiently on protein which is incorporated *naturally* into non-animal forms such as fresh vegetables, pulses and cereals. These not only provide a perfectly adequate amount of protein, but also supply the body with the fibre, carbohydrate and other essential nutrients which enable it to deal most efficiently with that protein, and which are vital to the body's general well-being and maintenance. The NACNE recommendations urge that plenty of healthy plant-derived protein should be included in the diet.

The shift towards carbohydrates

Unrefined carbohydrate such as whole cereals, vegetables, beans, peas, nuts and seeds (but *not* sugars, refined flours, white rice and other refined or highly processed starches such as crisps), are now of prime importance. Eat plenty of unrefined carbohydrate, it is now acknowledged, and a balanced proportion of other nutrients will almost invariably follow. In addition, disorders such as obesity, constipation, diverticular disease, and dental decay will also be avoided or greatly reduced.

There are several reasons for this. Unrefined carbohydrates are bulkier and therefore more filling; they do not dissolve tooth enamel; and they aid the smooth progress of food along the digestive tract.

A varied and interesting diet

In the light of all this, it is ironic that vegan or vegetarian cookbooks have often been apologetic in tone about the diet's supposed inadequacy. Tables of essential foods, daily requirements and instructions about sundry obscure vitamins and minerals often clutter the introductory pages of cookbooks, causing even the most determined would-be to turn away intimidated or bewildered. 'How on earth will I ever be able to stay healthy?' the readers wonder as they gaze at charts and tables intended to ensure that they 'balance' their diet. It is interesting to note, incidentally, that experts in Europe and the USA believe that the conventional concept of the 'balanced diet' is misleading and unnecessarily worrying. They suggest that it should be replaced by the idea of a *varied* diet which is open to the introduction of different and alternative foods, so the diet is opened up to a more healthy — and indeed exciting and delicious — range of ingredients and dishes. Of course, vegans do still have to make sure that their diets contain essential nutrients, but in my experience, the very fact that their eating habits are not those of society's 'norm' makes them more conscious of potential deficiencies, whereas those following a more conventional diet are often unwisely complacent about its nutritional adequacy. The one vitamin the vegan needs to keep an eye on is B12, which is found mainly in animal sources. It is quite easy to find foods which contain this essential element, howèver. Many of the basic ingredients used by vegans and vegetarians, such as yeast extracts, miso, and some soya milks, contain vitamin B12.

The additives problem

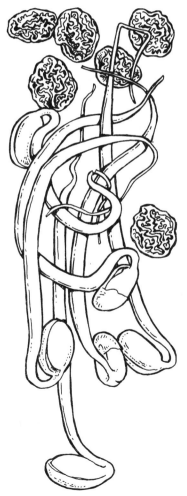

So far so good. We are becoming aware as never before about what is wrong with the Western diet. The only fly in the soup, it would seem, is that of trying to avoid the vast array of chemical additives, insecticide sprays and so forth to which modern farming and production techniques subject us via their products.

This is one major choice which is still largely denied us by the large, profit-seeking manufacturers and industrial concerns, who use additives in great quantities to 'improve' the flavour, texture, shelf-life and therefore the saleability of their products. It is currently estimated that the average person in Britain consumes the equivalent of ten aspirin tablets of additives alone per day, or well over 1 kilogramme (2.2 pounds), per year.[6] Many of these substances have been shown to produce harmful side-effects such as hyperactivity in children, headaches and depression and even, in a few cases, paralysis. The effects of other substances have not been tested at all.

But, again, things are beginning to change decisively as a result of the public's greater knowledge of and interest in the quality of the food they buy. Consumer demand has already prompted large chain stores not only to stock ranges of wholefoods and vegetarian preparations, but also to demand of their own suppliers that any additives contained in the foods are kept to an absolute minimum. Some of the larger stores check this in their own laboratories. Supermarkets are also beginning to provide the consumer with a choice between organically-grown vegetables and those which have been chemically sprayed and treated. If and when the demand is great enough, distribution outlets will multiply and the prices of organically-grown produce will become more competitive. These changes will only come about if consumers demand them — and the signs are optimistic.

The ecological aspect

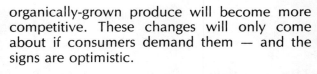

The ecological argument for the vegan diet is compelling. Veganism offers a simple yet comprehensive solution to the problems of global food shortages and of maintaining a balance of world resources with a relatively pollution-free environment.

Most of the wealthy countries of the world are in the northern hemisphere. They account for only 20 per cent of the earth's population, yet they consume approximately 90 per cent of the world's total energy resources. This means that the southern hemisphere which contains 80 per cent of the world population, mostly in Third World countries, receives a mere 10 per cent of those resources.

This gross imbalance happens because people in the affluent West want luxury goods such as fast cars and fashion clothing, and they want plenty of food. A massive proportion of those energy resources goes into the production of food, particularly that of meat and animal-derived products.

From the ecological point of view, meat production is remarkably inefficient despite the extremely high profit margins it creates for the high-technology farmer. For every pound of beef produced in the West, many times the amount of energy it provides has been used in its production. This takes the form of feed, growth promoters and other drugs which control the quantity and quality of the end product, heated farm buildings, medical treatment, fertilizers, seed, machinery to maintain pastureland, water, fuels, and so on. So the world's resources are being seriously depleted in order to satisfy people's craving for a great deal more meat and dairy products than are good for them. This state of affairs is not only morally unacceptable, it is also wholly avoidable. The same is true to a lesser extent of large scale chemically-aided crop production.

Efficiency of production

Another point is the astounding gulf between the production/energy efficiency of, say, the soya bean (the closest vegetable parallel to the protein contained in meat) and an animal foodstuff such as beef. A crop of soya beans will produce over twenty-eight times more protein per acre of land than beef production can. If that soya crop were to be cultivated organically, there would be a substantial energy gain. This is not to say, of course, that if everyone gave up eating animal-derived foods tomorrow the world's problems would be solved. But there is a lot of sense in eating *far less* of those products, or 'secondary' foodstuffs as they are termed, and turning to plant-based or 'primary' foods. This would help to cut down the rate at which we are using up the world's finite resources, and also restore the balance between what is taken from and what can be returned to the land. Lacto-vegetarianism is only a partial solution, since it still largely depends upon the provision of eggs and dairy foods, and thus upon intensive farming practices.

It would, of course, be naive to believe that the world's hungry millions would be fed if the greater part of the West's staple food came from plant sources. This is true in theory, but the issues of ownership, control and the often wasteful forces of the market economy might well continue to prevent such a situation, as is indicated by the present European food mountains.

The animal rights aspect

One of the more controversial arguments for eschewing foods and materials derived from animals is the issue of 'animal rights'. A growing number of people are taking up vegetarianism or veganism because of their concern about animals. Young people feel particularly strongly about this. According to one Gallup poll, the greatest concentration of non-meat eaters is found in the sixteen to twenty-four age group.[7]

Interpretations of animals' rights vary enormously, but all supporters have in common a respect for the lives of animals, and a conviction that they are entitled to a certain standard of welfare and treatment. Because animals cannot assert and defend their rights, they must be upheld for them by humans.

It is rare to find an active animal-rights' campaigner or sympathizer who actually eats meat and fish, and giving them up is not usually just a temporary fad. Most people make a permanent decision to give up animal products, and this often affects their families and friends as well. When one member of a family stops eating meat and fish, for example, others often follow suit and eat far less or give them up entirely.

The work of animal rights' groups

It is not really surprising that the debate about animal rights has become so inflamed over the past few years. The work of larger national and international organizations such as Greenpeace and Compassion In World Farming (which, it should be pointed out, do not represent any particular point on the political spectrum), have inspired the formation of many smaller groups with different degrees and types of commitment. Each is, nevertheless, dedicated to informing the public about what actually happens to animals subjected to modern farming techniques, from methods of conception and rearing to transportation and slaughter. The talks, lectures, seminars and literature they offer are aimed at making people aware of the disturbing reality behind the depictions of smiling, contented cows, pigs and hens which feature in advertising, product-packaging and the media.

The work of these groups and the publicity it

receives is gathering momentum, and public opinion is beginning to change, but widespread effects have not yet been felt. It is disheartening to learn of the proposed EEC legislation permitting a reduction of the space allotted to each battery hen by $1\frac{1}{2}$ square inches. The present battery cages are already so cramped that the hens cannot even ruffle their feathers. But this is not the place to go into the grim consequences for animals of present systems of farming and food-production. They could, sadly, fill a separate book.

The moral argument

The fourth main reason why many people adopt a vegan way of living involves a more personal decision than that taken in the interests of animal rights. The animal rights viewpoint is that all conscious life is equally valuable, and should be respected and preserved wherever reasonably possible. The moral argument is closely related to this, but does not necessarily bestow an equal value on *all* forms of conscious life. The central difference between the two arguments is that, whereas the former makes a claim for the independent rights of animals, the latter is predominantly concerned with the right or otherwise of human beings to inflict suffering on animals, whether or not their lives are intrinsically valuable.

These two persuasions often overlap, and thus the animal-rights sympathizer may nevertheless believe that the value of human life supersedes that of animals, and that animals can to some extent serve man. The distinction is worth pointing out, however, if only to draw attention to the varying degrees, and hence the essentially personal nature, of the decision to adopt veganism resulting from ethical considerations.

Unfortunately, many of the ethical arguments, delivered as they often are in lofty tones, have contributed to the idea that veganism is for cranks, 'hippies' or a certain elite. I myself am largely motivated by ethical concerns, and I think it is a great pity that some people still take this view. However, as the various alternative approaches to diet gain ground, the undesirably 'clubbish' image will inevitably diminish. After all, it is no longer a matter of 'conventional' versus 'vegetarian'. There is now a healthy plurality of values, ideas, beliefs and their associated practices, from macrobiotics and wholefoods through vegetarianism and veganism to the fruitarian diet, not to mention the various ethnic eating patterns and customs.

This book is about enjoying, preparing and eating good and healthy food. The vegan diet is one of the most healthy, interesting, imaginative, creative and appetizing ways of living and eating that one could wish for.

I hope that the ideas and alternatives in this book will stimulate those who simply want to expand their culinary repertoire a little, or to cut down on their consumption of meat, eggs and dairy products for reasons of health, or perhaps to entertain vegan guests at home or in a restaurant, as well as to those wishing to take up the vegan way of healthy living completely.

THE NATURE OF VEGANISM

This chapter attempts to answer some of the many questions people ask about veganism and what it involves in practical terms. Whether you are a would-be vegan, a vegetarian, a cook who just wants fresh ideas, or a thorough-going sceptic, I hope that it will clear up any grey areas for you.

Is it time-consuming?

The straight answer to this is 'No'. Vegan dishes need not take longer to prepare than any conventional recipe, and many dishes actually cut down on the time, effort and washing-up. Goodies like cheesecakes, ice-creams, mousses and creamy dressings are often simply a matter of blending ingredients in a blender or liquidizer and then baking them, chilling them or just serving them as they are. How much easier that is than separating and whisking eggs, folding in pre-whipped cream, or anxiously adding tiny quantities of oil to mayonnaise so that it does not curdle.

The cooking of pulses is probably the most time-consuming aspect of vegan food preparation, but even this takes no longer than cooking many kinds of meat. Another bonus is that you do not have to trim, cut, bone, or coat in flour, as you do with so many meat dishes. Dried pulses can either be soaked overnight or hot-soaked for an hour or so in freshly boiled water (as explained on page 183), then boiled for

30–60 minutes before being added to the dish. Again, the actual labour required is negligible — and this applies also to dishes based on nuts, grains, cereals, seeds or the more quickly cooked pulses like lentils or mung beans.

Cakes should also be given a mention here, not least because many people think it is impossible to make a cake without eggs. As I will show later in the book, vegan cooks can make delicious cakes and the process is often quicker and simpler than following a conventional recipe.

Surely vegan food gets boring?

Nothing could be further from the truth. Even before I became vegan, I was impressed by the huge variety of different flavours, textures and possible combinations in the *vegetarian* diet. When I became interested in vegan cooking, I discovered that, paradoxically, there were even *more* culinary possibilities. Apart from all the different pulses, nuts, grains, cereals and seeds one can use, I have found a whole range of ways to use tofu (a soya bean curd) for anything from starters, salads, casseroles and stir-fries to cream sauces, soufflés and pasta.

Then there are all the vegan cheeses, which are a delight to experiment with. The prospect of giving up cow's milk, cheeses and other dairy products used to seem daunting, I must admit. I could not believe that there was any other base for cheese than cow's milk. Little did I realize just how much more I was to gain than I was to give up! Not only are vegan cheeses delicious and nutritious, but they are quick to make too. You can choose from delicately-flavoured or strong 'mature' types; some are of a soft, spreading consistency, others have a crumbly ricotta texture, or there are harder, firmer types which are good for slicing, grilling or grating for use in sandwiches, salads, on toast or as toppings for vegetables and main courses. But more of all this in the 'Vegan Dairy' section!

Is it difficult to balance the daily diet?

We have already seen that there is less chance of suffering malnutrition or of developing diseases on a vegan diet than on a conventional one.

Vitamin B12, as I have pointed out, is present chiefly in animal-derived foods, so this is the one nutritional element that the vegan should consciously include in his or her diet. The vitamin does occur naturally in seaweeds like kelp, and in miso (a fermented soyabean paste which is frequently used in vegan and vegetarian cooking), as well as in widely used, commercially made products like vegetable spreads and stocks, yeast extracts, brewer's yeast, margarines and certain brands of soya milk.

It is sometimes said that the vegan child and pregnant or lactating mother must take care to consume enough calcium. However, this also applies to the same 'special categories' of people on a conventional diet. A number of foods, such as almonds, sesame seeds and brazil nuts, are rich in the mineral. The vegan child or mother can eat extra amounts of these foods, just as the conventional mother or child has more dairy milk or other calcium-rich foods.

It might be salutory to end the discussion of this particular question with the example of the Caucasians and Hunzakuts. These peoples live on an almost exclusively vegan diet, and continue to hold the world records for average longevity. It is not uncommon for them to live for more than 100 years and still be relatively fit. Some reach 120 or 130 years, and sometimes more. Although the clear air and pure water of their mountain habitat doubtless contributes to their long lifespan, the healthy diet they have traditionally followed is acknowledged to be the major factor in maintaining their extraordinary degree of strength, fitness and general well-being to such an old age.

Do you have to buy a lot of specialist equipment for vegan cooking?

Again, the answer is 'No'. True, a grinder/liquidizer is a boon for recipes which involve grinding nuts, making breadcrumbs or liquidizing soups and whipped desserts, but this is standard equipment in most kitchens nowadays, and hardly represents a major financial outlay.

A food processor is always handy for chopping vegetables, or as a roomy alternative to the liquidizer for mixing cheesecake fillings, creamy desserts and the like. As far as making cheeses is concerned, the only essential equipment is a saucepan and, in the case of softer cream, curd and cottage cheeses, a colander and a piece of muslin. You need the same equipment for making tofu, plus a sieve and one or two weights such as full jam-jars.

So the equipment for vegan cookery is fairly standard, though any labour-saving devices you can afford are welcome, just as they are for any cook. Ice-cream makers, for example, give a superb light and creamy texture to the various types of ice-cream which can be made, but the same applies if you are making dairy ice-creams, and you can certainly manage without one.

Will it cost a lot?

This question always astonishes me, yet it is understandable when one remembers the gimmicky and high-priced health-food stores which sprang up during the 1970s. Nowadays, however, people are generally more interested in having a healthy diet, which has prompted many more retail outlets to respond to the demand for natural, unprocessed foods at competitive prices.

A healthy vegan diet is actually far less expensive than one which includes a substantial proportion of meat and animal products. That instant vegan snack, a tin of baked beans, for example, provides more protein than an equal weight of steak at a fraction of the cost (and without the high saturated fat and cholesterol content of that steak).

Not only are plant-derived foods less expensive to buy than foods taken from animals (even relative luxuries like almonds and pine-kernels still compare favourably against equal weights of many popular cuts of meat), but they are also generally less perishable and so there is less wastage. Staples like pulses, nuts, seeds and cereals, as well as the new freeze-dried tofu, have a lengthy shelf-life and, importantly, do not run the risk of harbouring poisonous bacteria such as salmonella or butolinum, as does animal produce and fish. Moreover, the pulses are doubly economical; not only are they inexpensive, but they expand when they are soaked so a little goes a long way.

Fresh vegetables and fruits are the only major item in the vegan diet with a fairly short storage life, but there is no reason why vegans should spend more on these foods than anyone else. Even if you want to include some of the more exotic and expensive varieties such as kiwi fruits, mooli or mange-touts, which are now on offer in many greengrocers and supermarkets, you will still be saving by not buying meat. And none of these foods is essential to the vegan diet — no single fruit or vegetable is.

But wouldn't I have to give up cakes and creamy desserts?

I think one of the biggest misconceptions people have about a vegan diet, is that it means giving up all those marvellous goodies which make life worth living, such as creamy cakes, sauces and dressings, ice-cream, and milk-shakes. There would be no one more stricken by misery than myself if this were so, but fortunately it is not. The truth is that there are vegan versions — and superb ones at that — for virtually any conventional dish or indulgence that one can imagine.

Thanks to the versatility of basic vegan foodstuffs like nuts, seeds, and especially the soya bean with its ability to be woven into meat-like textures, to be converted into milk or to produce a delicate and endlessly adaptable curd called tofu, vegan *haute cuisine* can be just as temptingly attractive and delicious as that of Carrier or Cordon Bleu, without the disadvantages and hazards to health of much conventional or gourmet cooking.

Another thing I have noticed, from my own experience and that of others, is that the less one eats animal products, the more one finds them over-rich and, in the case of dairy products, positively sickly in comparison to their vegan equivalents. This is perhaps not surprising in the light of the fact that nine out of ten people are to some extent allergic to the lactose and casein content of milk intended in nature for calves. In fact, until very recently in terms of human evolution, the human diet consisted predominantly of plant foods, punctuated only occasionally by a dose of hunted meat, which was of course wild and therefore much less fatty than that of our present intensively-farmed, chemically treated animal.

All of this has changed drastically over the years, and particularly since the middle of this century. People now have affluent tastes, and they are loath to give them up. But, as I hope this book will demonstrate, there is no need to give up the things we enjoy in order to avoid the risks associated with the modern Western diet. The vegan approach to diet allows us to retain these tastes while offering us the bonus of discovering new ones and of enjoying good health at the same time.

Isn't veganism terribly anti-social?

At one time this would have been fair comment. Only a decade or so ago even lacto-vegetarianism was practically unknown in polite society, and was usually thought to be some form of eccentric or cult practice. Now, however, with a fast-rising number of people taking up vegetarianism in Western societies (in Britain alone there are at present around 1.5 million and this number is increasing all the time), information about and interest in this type of diet has spread to such an extent that its deserved status as a sane and perfectly respectable, *un*restrictive approach to living is at last becoming firmly established.

The same can now be said of veganism. As people have come to realize the damages of eating cholesterol-rich foods such as meat and dairy produce, so there has been new recognition for veganism as a sensible and healthy way to eat.

This recognition has prompted many lacto-ovo-vegetarians to take the further step to veganism, while many other people are simply trying to cut down on their intake of animal-derived foods.

For evidence of this one has only to look at the increasing availability of vegan dishes, not only in wholefood restaurants, but also in a growing number of otherwise conventional eating places. This trend is even more noticeable with commercially-made vegan products. Not only are these more plentiful and varied in health food stores, but they are now finding their way into the large chain stores and supermarkets. No longer are such foods presented in an uninspiring manner. They are being packaged and promoted as colourful, attractive and eminently pleasurable commodities. Soya milk, tofu, pulses and even 'instant' or pre-cooked vegan canned and packet meals (whether or not they are referred to as vegan), can be found amongst the displays of the most well-known stores.

As people become more and more aware of the potential of vegan cooking, they find entertaining guests of mixed dietary persuasion less daunting, too. Instead of feeling that they have to cook something separate for the vegans, they realize that they can plan a menu which will please and satisfy vegans and non-vegans alike.

As I said earlier, this book is not preaching complete conversion to a vegan diet for everyone tomorrow. It is intended to encourage people to try vegan cookery, thus helping those wishing to change completely to vegan foods to acquaint themselves with the many possibilities and delights open to them in a positive and imaginative way, and also providing those who are simply interested in healthy culinary alternatives with a whole new range of foods and ideas.

References

1. Colin Tudge: *The Food Connection* (B.B.C., 1985) p. 48.
2. *The NACNE Report* (National Advisory Committee on Nutrition Education, 1983) p. 7.
3. *The Food and Health Campaign* (B.B.C. booklet, 1985) p. 3.
4. Colin Tudge op cit p. 67.
5. Quoted, for example, by Joan Maynard at the Labour Party Conference, 1985.
6. *Food For Thought* (Health Education Council booklet, 1985) p. 14.
7. *Animal or Vegetable?* Quoted in *Observer* report, 6. 10. 1985.

THE VEGAN DAIRY

The vegan dairy contains many appetizing alternatives to conventional dairy foods. These alternatives are not only better suited to the physiological workings and needs of the human body, but they actually offer a wider range of types and flavours to choose from. Vegan dairy products are also just as adaptable and versatile in cooking as their non-vegan counterparts.

Milks

Soya milk is now sold in supermarkets as well as in health-food shops. Each brand of soya milk has its own subtly different flavour, so it is worth trying a few different ones to see which you prefer, or just for the sake of variation. Instructions for making your own soya milk are given as 'Stage 1' of the instructions for making tofu (see page 179).

Milks can also be made from nuts, seeds, cereals and soya flour. I have given a couple of recipes which provide, among other benefits, a good measure of calcium. But try experimenting yourself with many other possible flavours and combinations.

Margarines and shortenings

A number of vegan margarines are now available. Suma sunflower margarine is, in my opinion, the most tasty soft-spreading margarine, but other brands are starting to follow suit with their own versions. Harder margarines for cooking include those made by

Vitaseig and Granose. Nutter is a useful solid vegetable shortening which is particularly good for making firmer cutting cheeses, whilst the product Suenut provides an excellent alternative to the animal-derived suet for puddings, dumplings and so forth.

Butter spreads

You can make your own butters very easily, by grinding nuts or seeds and mixing them with enough oil to give a spreading consistency. An increasing range of these spreads and butters is to be found ready-made on the shelves of wholefood and other stores.

Creams

These can be made using a number of different basic ingredients, separately or combined. Nuts, creamed coconut, tofu, soya milk or soymilk powder can all be transformed into light and tempting creams, from the thinner, pouring types to the thick spooning varieties. Again, I have suggested a few, but you will find it enjoyable and rewarding to conjure up your own, too.

Cheeses

These 'dairy products' comprise one of the most open-ended and pleasurable areas of vegan cooking or preparation. Making vegan cheeses is always simple and straightforward, but you can create so many flavours, textures and consistencies that I can only put forward a few basic suggestions and ideas if they are not to take over the whole book!

Try adding extra ingredients to your soft or hard cheeses, such as celery and caraway seed; chopped walnuts and dates; ground aniseed with grated lemon rind; celery seed and raisins; fresh sage and chive or onion; and so on.

Yoghurt

I find that home-made soya milk yoghurt is far preferable to the shop varieties. It is also much more economical. Use a commercially-made yoghurt culture and a wide-necked thermos flask or yoghurt maker for the first batch. Subsequent batches can be cultured from 2–3 tablespoons reserved from the previous one. Apart from its culinary usefulness and pleasant taste, soya yoghurt is also a very efficient aid to digestion.

Eggs

Egg-based conventional dishes such as omelettes and soufflés can be translated into vegan forms by substituting tofu. You could try Broccoli Tofu Soufflé (see page 60), or tofu scrambled with a little margarine, ground turmeric and soy sauce, on toast. In recipes where a binding agent is needed, a tablespoon each of soya flour and arrowroot will perform that function and provide similar nutritional values to those of an egg (minus the egg's cholesterol and saturated fat content).

Egg-whites can be replaced by agar-agar dissolved in boiling water and then cooled, for making glazes or for royal icing. It is even possible to buy powdered meringue from some bakers, but as these are chemically produced simulations of meringue, and as there are so many alternative desserts, cakes and puddings in the vegan repertoire, I would suggest that there really is no need to use such a product.

Milks

Almond and Oatmeal Milk

3 oz (75g) ground almonds
3 oz (75g) fine *or* medium oatmeal
$\frac{3}{4}$ pint (425ml) water

Place the almonds and oatmeal in a liquidizer goblet and pour in the water. Blend thoroughly, pour into a jug or bowl and leave to stand for 30 minutes. Then press through a sieve, reserving pulp for other uses such as adding to breakfast muesli, porridge or cake mixtures. Keep covered and chilled.

Cashew and Sesame Milk

3 oz (75g) cashew nut
  pieces
1 oz (25g) sesame seeds
12 fl oz (350ml) water

Grind the cashews and seeds finely together in a grinder. Tip into a liquidizer goblet and pour in the water. Blend thoroughly two or three times. Leave to stand for 30 minutes, then press through a sieve. Store and use as Almond and Oatmeal Milk (page 31).

Creams

Whipped Cream

½ pint (275ml) water
4 oz (100g) soya-milk
  powder
2 tablespoons sunflower
  oil
2 tablespoons maple
  syrup
1½ teaspoons natural
  vanilla essence
2 teaspoons freshly-
  squeezed lemon juice
1 oz (25g) vegan soft
  margarine

Place the water and soya-milk powder in a liquidizer and blend thoroughly. Add the oil, syrup, vanilla essence and lemon juice and blend again.

Beat the soft margarine in a bowl until light and fluffy. Add the soya milk mixture a little at a time, beating after each addition until a light, soft, whipped-cream texture results.

Note: Some soya-milk powders already contain sugar. If using this type, omit the maple syrup and only add this or any other sweetening if necessary after tasting.

Tofu Whipped Cream

¼ pint (150ml) concentrated soya milk
¼ pint (150ml) soya milk
1 rounded tablespoon arrowroot
1 tablespoon either: honey, *or* soft brown sugar *or* maple syrup
1 vanilla pod
2 oz (50g) silken or firm tofu, crumbled or mashed
1½ oz (37g) vegan soft margarine

Place the milks in a pan. Put the arrowroot and sweetening in a measuring jug and stir in a little of the milk mixture to form a thin paste. Add the vanilla pod to the pan and heat the milk to near boiling point. Remove from heat, cover and leave to stand for 30 minutes to one hour. After this time, remove the vanilla pod, reheat the milk to boiling point and add to the arrowroot, stirring briskly. Return the mixture to the pan and continue to stir until thickened. Remove from heat and allow to cool completely, then mix in the tofu and liquidize.

Beat the margarine in a medium/large mixing bowl until fluffy. Add the tofu and milk mixture a little at a time, beating well after each addition to ensure a soft and light cream.

Note: Choose your tofu according to the desired thickness you want — silken tofu will produce a slightly more fluid consistency than will the firmer types.

Cashew Nut Cream

4 oz (100g) cashew nuts, ground
6 fl oz (175ml) soya milk
1 dessertspoon sunflower oil
1 teaspoon maple syrup (optional)

Place all the ingredients in a liquidizer and blend until smooth. If storing in a refrigerator before use, stir before pouring, as the surface sometimes thickens a little when chilled or left to stand for a while.

Coconut Cream

4 oz (100g) creamed coconut, grated
8 fl oz (225ml) freshly boiled water
1–2 teaspoons maple syrup, honey *or* sugar (optional)

Place the grated creamed coconut in a liquidizer. Pour over the hot water and liquidize until well blended to a light, creamy consistency. Taste, add sweetening if desired, and blend once more. Pour into a jug or container, cover and allow to cool, then chill in refrigerator. Stir a little before serving.

Note: This particular cream tends to thicken as it chills, so can actually be made with less water than specified (say 5–6 fl oz or 150–175ml), then chilled and served as a vegan version of whipped double cream, to be spooned onto desserts when eaten, or as garnish.

Soured Cream

6 oz (175g) silken tofu
3 tablespoons sunflower oil
1 dessertspoon lemon juice
A good pinch of soft brown sugar
A small pinch of salt

Blend all ingredients thoroughly in a liquidizer until smooth and creamy.

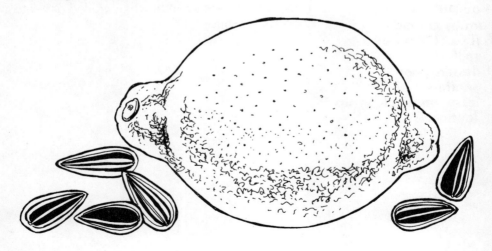

Cheeses

Basic Vegan Cheese (A firm, cutting cheese)

Makes approximately 9 oz (250g)

2½ oz (62g) Nutter
2½ oz (62g) vegan hard margarine (such as Granose, Vitaseig)
1 teaspoon yeast extract (or to taste)
4 oz (100g) soya flour

Melt the Nutter and margarine in a pan and stir in the yeast extract. Add the soya flour and mix well to a smooth consistency. Pour into a suitable sized container and leave to cool, then chill until completely set. To remove, run a sharp, pointed knife around the edges of the dish, invert over a plate and sharply knock the base. Repeat the procedure if necessary until the cheese comes away.

This cheese has a similar firmness and consistency to that of cheddar, and can be used for similar purposes. It can be cut for sandwiches, grated into salads, grilled on toast, used as a topping for baked casseroles, vegetables, and snacks, or used to make sauces. And of course, it is good eaten by itself!

Soy-nut Cheese

Makes 9¼ oz (262g)

3 oz (75g) Nutter
1 oz (25g) vegan hard margarine
2 oz (50g) cashew nuts
1½ oz (37g) walnuts
2 oz (50g) soya flour
½–1 teaspoon yeast extract

This is one version, but you can use your imagination to make many others. I chose cashews and walnuts because I think the combination of tastes and textures makes the cheese full-flavoured, rich and creamy, but other combinations are distinctive in other ways.

Melt the margarine and Nutter in a pan. Meanwhile, grind the cashews and walnuts together in a grinder and mix with the soya flour in a bowl. Stir the yeast extract into the melted mixture, then add the dry ingredients, half at a time, mixing well after each addition until evenly blended.

Turn into a suitable container, allow to cool, then chill for at least an hour before turning out.

Basic Cottage Cheese

Makes approximately 6 oz (175g)

1½ pints (850ml) soya milk
2 tablespoons freshly squeezed lemon juice
1 teaspoon cider vinegar

Line a colander with a piece of muslin and set over a large bowl. Gently heat the soya milk in a pan with the other ingredients, stirring occasionally, until the mixture can be seen to separate into curds and whey (it is best to let the mixture get quite hot to ensure full separation). Pour into the lined colander to strain the whey off into the bowl. Wait for a few minutes until a soft but fairly firm curd is left, then transfer the contents of the muslin to a suitable container, season to taste with a little salt if desired, and keep covered and chilled until ready to use.

Variations can be made on this and other vegan soft cheeses by changing the curdling agent. For example, you can use all vinegar, or supplement the lemon juice with a tablespoon or two of orange or grapefruit juice. Also try adding herbs such as chives or mint; spices; seeds; garlic; chopped nuts; fruits such as pineapple, apricot, raisins; or combinations of these, to the resulting cheese.

Cream Cheese

Makes 8 oz (225g)

1 pint (575ml) concentrated soya milk
2 tablespoons freshly squeezed lemon juice

Proceed as for basic cottage cheese above. This is good eaten on its own, or to use as a base for many dishes such as uncooked cheesecakes; or pâtés and spreads. It can be mixed with vegetables such as cooked, chopped spinach and mushrooms and garlic as a filling for cannelloni, lasagne, or pancakes.

Yoghurt Cheese

This is simple, refreshing and superb with, for example, fresh mint and chopped cucumber, or mixed with chopped fresh fruits (especially soft fruits).

Place a square of muslin in a bowl, pour or ladle in a quantity of soya yoghurt (yoghurt made from concentrated soya milk is, of course, quicker in producing the cheese), bring the corners of the muslin together, wind and tie in a loose knot. Either hang this over a sink or place in a colander set over a bowl with a weight (such as a plate with a full jar or other heavy object on it) pressing down on the muslin bag. Leave for at least 5–6 hours and preferably overnight, for excess moisture to seep out and leave a thick, creamy, but light soft cheese. Transfer to a covered container and store in the refrigerator until required.

Curd Cheese

Makes approximately 1lb 2oz (500g)

6 oz (175ml) soya flour
½ pint (275ml) cold water
1 pint (575ml) boiling water
Juice of 1½ lemons
A pinch of nutmeg

Sift the soya flour into a large saucepan and gradually add the cold water, mixing to a smooth paste. Pour over the boiling water a little at a time to ensure that no lumps form, then bring gently to the boil, stirring constantly. Simmer for 5–6 minutes, stirring frequently to prevent any sticking. Remove from heat, add the lemon juice and nutmeg, stir again and allow to cool slightly. Stand a colander in a large bowl and line it with muslin. Pour the soya flour mixture into the lined colander to allow the whey to drain through. After about 5–7 minutes, pick up the corners of the muslin and twist together gently to squeeze out any excess whey. Turn the curd which is left in the muslin into a suitably sized container and keep chilled in refrigerator.

Add flavours as for cottage cheese (opposite), if desired.

Tofu and Nut Soft Cheese

Makes about 14 oz (400g)

1 × 10½ oz (287g) pkt silken tofu
4–5 oz (100–150g) chopped mixed nuts, ground
2 teaspoons freshly squeezed lemon *or* orange juice

Mix the tofu well with the ground mixed nuts and juice. Flavour, if wanted, with seasoning, garlic, herbs or a few drops of soy sauce.

This is good with salads, or as a base for dips, spreads, or flan fillings. It can also be mixed with cooked rice and other ingredients and used as a stuffing for vegetables.

Tofu Ricotta Cheese

Makes 1 lb (450g)

8 oz (225g) firm tofu
8 oz (225g) silken tofu
A squeeze of fresh lemon juice
A small pinch of salt (optional)

Mash the firm and silken tofu together with the lemon juice, and salt if required. (If a coarser ricotta texture is wanted, simply crumble the firm tofu into the previously whisked silken tofu and fold in. Then stir in the lemon juice and season to taste.)

For an example of how to use, see Aubergine and Brazil Nut Bake (page 78).

Seed and Nut Soft Cheese

Makes 8–9 oz
  (225–250g)

**2 oz (50g) chopped
  mixed nuts**
**1 oz (25g) sunflower
  seeds**
1 oz (25g) sesame seeds
**2 oz (50g) soft
  sunflower margarine**
**3 tablespoons sunflower
  oil**
2 oz (50g) soya flour

Spread the nuts and seeds on a baking tray and toast under a medium/hot grill for 5–7 minutes, turning occasionally, until lightly browned. Allow to cool, then grind finely.

Heat the margarine and oil in a pan and stir in the ground nuts and seeds until evenly blended. Add the soya flour, mix in well and turn into a container to cool. Keep covered in refrigerator.

Note: I think this cheese is superb as it is, but one can of course add seasonings, herbs, garlic and so forth for extra flavour if desired. It can be used as a spread or dip, or combined with cooked millet or rice, onion and so on, and used as a filling for baked vegetables.

Mixed Seed Soft Cheese

Makes 10–11 oz
  (275–300g)

**2 tablespoons sunflower
  seeds**
**2 tablespoons pumpkin
  seeds**
**1 tablespoon poppy
  seeds**
**1 tablespoon sesame
  seeds**
**1 level teaspoon
  caraway seeds**
**5 tablespoons
  sunflower, safflower
  or corn oil**
1 oz (25g) soya flour
**8–9 tablespoons apple
  juice**

Mix all the seeds together and grind finely. Heat the oil slightly in a pan and mix in the ground seeds and soya flour. Add the apple juice a tablespoon at a time, beating well after each addition until a soft, creamy consistency is obtained.

Note: This is a particularly light, mellow-tasting soft cheese. It can be served as a delicious and unusual soft spread or dip.

Chestnut Cheese

*Makes 13–14 oz
   (375–400g)*

**3 oz (75g) dried
   chestnuts
1 bay leaf
2 oz (50g) Nutter
1 oz (25g) vegan hard
   margarine
½ teaspoon yeast extract
2 teaspoons soy sauce
2 oz (50g) soya flour
A pinch mustard
   powder**

Rinse the chestnuts well. Place them in a pan with the bay leaf and double their height of water. Bring to the boil and simmer for 1–1¼ hours. Then drain, remove the bay leaf and mash well with a fork or a puréeing appliance. Melt the Nutter and margarine over a gentle heat (this could be done in the same pan as the chestnuts, so long as you keep stirring, to prevent the mashed or puréed chestnuts from sticking, and to blend the ingredients evenly).

When melted, stir in the yeast extract until dissolved, then add the remaining ingredients and beat together thoroughly. Season to taste if desired and turn the mixture into a suitable container to cool. Chill in the refrigerator for at least 2 hours before turning out.

Sesame-almond Cheese

*Makes 9–10 oz
   (250–275g)*

**2½ oz (62g) almond nibs
   or pieces
1 oz (25g) sesame seeds
2 oz (50g) Nutter
2 oz (50g) vegan hard
   margarine
½–1 teaspoon yeast
   extract
2 oz (50g) soya flour**

Grind the almonds and sesame seeds together. Melt the Nutter and margarine in a pan and stir in the yeast extract. Add the ground nuts and seeds and the soya flour. Mix well until evenly blended. Turn into a suitable-sized container, cover and allow to cool. Chill for at least 3 hours before turning out.

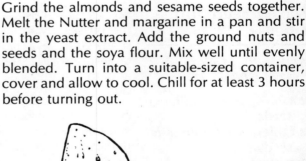

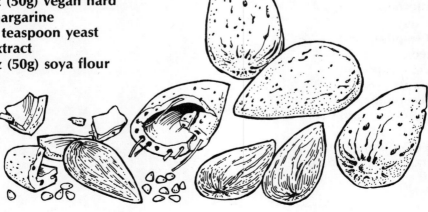

SOUPS

Vegetable Stock

1 large onion
2 sticks celery
2 carrots
1 large parsnip *or*
    potato
2 bay leaves
2 tablespoons chopped
    fresh parsley
3 pints (1.75 litres)
    water

Wash, peel or trim and roughly chop all the vegetables. Place in a saucepan with the water, bay leaves and parsley. Bring to the boil and simmer for $1\frac{1}{4}$–$1\frac{1}{2}$ hours. Allow to cool a little, then use a sieve to strain off the stock. When it has cooled completely, the stock can be stored in the refrigerator for up to 3 or 4 days, or frozen until required.

Cream of Melon and Almond Soup

Serves 4–6

2 small and very ripe
    honeydew *or* similar
    sweet melons
$\frac{1}{4}$ pint (150ml)
    concentrated soya
    milk
4–5 tablespoons white
    wine
3 oz (75g) ground
    almonds
Toasted, flaked
    almonds to garnish

Halve the melons and remove the seeds. Scrape out the flesh into a large bowl and roughly chop it. Add the remaining ingredients, mix well and blend in a liquidizer until smooth. Chill for at least an hour, then stir before pouring into serving bowls (a little ordinary soya milk can be added at this stage if a thinner consistency is desired). Garnish with toasted, flaked almonds scattered on the surface of the soup.

Tomato and Dill Soup

Serves 4–6

1 lb (450g) tomatoes, skinned and quartered
1 bunch spring onions or 1 medium onion, roughly chopped
1 clove garlic, chopped
1 tablespoon chopped, fresh dill *or* 2 teaspoons dried dill
¾ pint (425ml) vegetable stock (see page 41)
¾ pint (425ml) tomato juice
¼ teaspoon allspice
1 tablespoon freshly squeezed lemon juice
Freshly ground black pepper and salt
To garnish: a sprig of dill, *or* 1 tablespoon chopped spring onion tops, *or* a few spoonsful vegan soured cream (see page 34)

Place all the ingredients in a large saucepan and bring to the boil. Simmer for 30 minutes. Allow to cool, then purée in a blender or food processor, or by rubbing through a sieve. Season to taste, garnish, and serve hot or chilled. Croûtons are also good with this soup.

Note: For variation, try adding the finely grated rind of half an orange.

Celery, Apple and Barley Soup

Serves 4–6

10 oz (275g) roughly chopped celery
1 large *or* 2 small leeks, roughly chopped
1 tablespoon vegetable oil
2 crisp dessert apples, peeled, cored and chopped
1 level teaspoon celery seed
1 pint (575ml) apple juice
1 pint (575ml) water
1 oz (25g) pot barley, rinsed thoroughly
Black pepper and salt
Toasted barley kernels *or* flakes to garnish

Gently sauté the celery and leek in the oil for 3–4 minutes, then add the apples and celery seed, cover and continue to cook for a further 2–3 minutes. Pour in the apple juice and water, bring gently to the boil and stir in the pot barley. Simmer, covered, for 50–60 minutes, stirring occasionally. Then remove from heat and allow to cool slightly. Liquidize the soup in a blender or food processor, season to taste and reheat to serve. Garnish with a light sprinkling of barley kernels or flakes, which you have toasted under a moderate grill, turning frequently, for a few minutes.

Spiced Spinach and Lentil Soup

Serves 4–6

6 oz (175g) continental lentils
1 tablespoon vegetable oil
1 teaspoon cumin seeds
1 teaspoon mustard seeds
1 teaspoon garam masala
1 fresh green *or* red chilli, finely chopped, *or* ½ teaspoon chilli powder
1 medium/large onion, finely chopped
1 clove garlic, crushed
1 teaspoon basil
1 teaspoon freshly grated root ginger
½ teaspoon ground bay leaves, *or* 2 whole bay leaves
2 pints (1.25 litres) water or vegetable stock
12 oz (350g) spinach, blanched and chopped finely
1 tablespoon soy sauce
1 tablespoon freshly squeezed lemon juice
Black pepper and salt
2–3 tablespoons soya yoghurt (see page 30) (optional)

Remove any stones or grit from the lentils and rise thoroughly in a sieve. Heat the oil in a large saucepan and fry the lentils with the seeds and spices for 3–4 minutes, tossing frequently with a spoon to prevent burning. Add the onion, garlic and fresh chilli if using, the basil and ginger, and cook for a further 2–3 minutes. Add the bay leaves and water or stock, the chopped spinach and the soy sauce. Bring to the boil and simmer for 50–60 minutes until the lentils are tender. Stir in the lemon juice, remove from heat and allow to cool slightly. Liquidize about *half* of the soup. Return to the pan and season to taste.

This soup is superb on its own, but as a variation or if a subtle cooling effect is required to complement the taste of the spices, add the yoghurt, reheat and serve with croutons and/or a swirl of soya yoghurt.

Carrot and Peanut Soup

Serves 4-6

1 oz (25g) vegan
  margarine
1 tablespoon oil
1½ lb (675g) carrots,
  roughly chopped
3 sticks celery, roughly
  chopped
1 medium onion,
  chopped
2 teaspoons ground
  coriander
5 oz (150g) peanuts
1¾ pints (1 litre)
  vegetable stock
1 bay leaf
2 heaped tablespoons
  peanut butter
Black pepper and salt
A few chopped roasted
  peanuts to garnish

Melt the margarine with the oil in a large covered saucepan and cook the carrots, celery and onion over a low heat for 7–8 minutes until the onion is softened but not browned. Add the peanuts and coriander and continue to cook for a further 2–3 minutes. Pour in the stock and add the bay leaf. Bring to the boil and simmer gently for 35–40 minutes, stirring occasionally. Remove from the heat and allow to cool slightly. Then liquidize, return to the pan and stir in the peanut butter until evenly blended. Season to taste.

Serve hot, garnished with a sprinkling of chopped roasted peanuts, with warm crusty bread rolls.

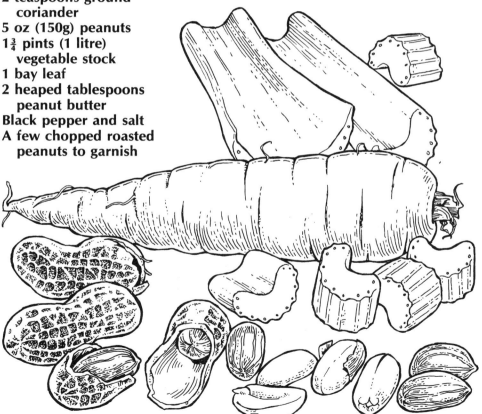

Watercress and Orange Soup

Serves 4

1½ oz (37g) vegan
   margarine
8 oz (225g) watercress,
   chopped
4 tablespoons freshly
   squeezed orange
   juice
Finely grated rind half
   an orange
1 pint (575ml) soya
   yoghurt
Black pepper and salt
Sprigs of watercress to
   garnish

Melt the margarine in a pan and add the chopped watercress. Cover and cook over a low heat for 6–7 minutes until softened. Allow to cool, then place in a liquidizer or food processor with the remaining ingredients. Blend thoroughly, season to taste and chill the soup for at least an hour before serving, garnished with small sprigs of fresh watercress.

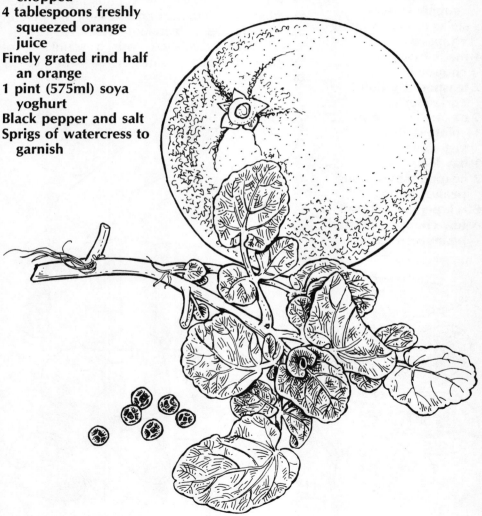

Parsnip and Sesame Soup

Serves 4–6

- 1 large onion, roughly chopped
- 1 oz (25g) vegan margarine
- 1 tablespoon oil
- 1 lb (450g) parsnips, peeled and roughly chopped
- 1 teaspoon dried rosemary
- 1 pint (575ml) water
- 1 bay leaf
- 2 oz (50g) ground cashew nuts
- 2 oz (50g) ground sesame seeds
- 1 pint (575ml) soya milk
- $\frac{1}{2}$ pint (275ml) apple juice
- Black pepper and salt
- 1–2 teaspoons whole, toasted sesame seeds to garnish

Heat the margarine and oil in a large saucepan and sauté the onion for 3–4 minutes until soft but not browned. Stir in the parsnips and rosemary and continue to cook, covered, for a further 4–5 minutes. Add the water and bay leaf, bring to the boil and simmer for 25–30 minutes. Then remove bay leaf, stir in the ground cashew nuts, sesame seeds, soya milk and apple juice, and liquidize in a blender or food processor until smooth and creamy (more apple juice or water may be added if a thinner consistency is desired).

To serve, reheat, stirring occasionally and taking care not to boil the soup, and season to taste with black pepper and salt. Garnish with a sprinkling of whole toasted sesame seeds.

Courgette and Tarragon Bisque

Serves 4–6

4 oz (100g) mushrooms, wiped and roughly chopped
1½ oz (37g) vegan margarine
1 lb (450g) courgettes, topped and tailed, washed and thickly sliced
2 teaspoons dried tarragon, *or* 1 tablespoon chopped, fresh tarragon
¾ pint (425g) vegetable stock
¾ pint (425g) soya milk
1 tablespoon sherry
A pinch or two of nutmeg
Black pepper and salt
Concentrated soya milk and chopped fresh tarragon *or* parsley to garnish

Melt the margarine in a large saucepan and sauté the mushrooms, covered for about 10 minutes over a low heat. Add the courgettes and tarragon and continue cooking for a further 4–5 minutes. Pour in the stock, bring gently to the boil and simmer for 8–10 minutes. Add soya milk, sherry and nutmeg, heat to near boiling point, then remove from heat, cover and allow to cool slightly. Liquidize the soup until smooth in a blender or liquidizer, or by rubbing through a sieve. Season to taste and reheat (but do not boil) before serving. Pour into bowls and garnish with very thin slices of courgette or mushroom, or with a swirl of concentrated soya milk and a sprinkling of fresh, chopped tarragon or parsley.

PÂTÉS AND STARTERS

Cheese-nut Pâté

Serves 4–6

**8 oz (225g) basic
    cottage cheese (see
    page 36)**
**1 oz (25g) vegan
    margarine**
**2 level teaspoons
    wholegrain mustard**
**4 oz (100g) salted
    peanuts, rinsed,
    patted dry and finely
    chopped or crushed**
**1 level teaspoon
    caraway seeds**
**4 oz (100g) grated hard
    cheese (see page 35)**
Black pepper and salt
**Parsley sprigs and
    wedges of lemon to
    garnish**

Cream the cottage cheese with the margarine until light and fluffy. Beat in the mustard, then fold in the rest of the ingredients. Divide between 4–6 individual ramekin dishes and put these on plates with a garnish of parsley sprigs and a wedge of lemon.

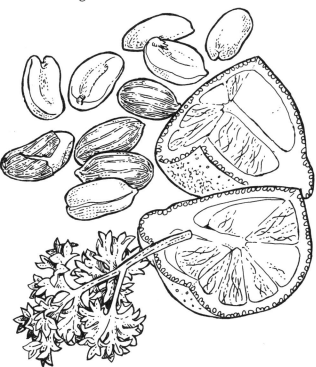

50

Vegan Vitality

Aubergine and Pine-nut Starter

Serves 4–6

2 large aubergines
3–4 cloves garlic, very thinly sliced
4 tomatoes, skinned and finely chopped
1 oz (25g) currants
1½ oz (37g) pine-kernels, toasted
2 tablespoons fresh parsley, finely chopped
1 teaspoon soy sauce
1 dessertspoon olive oil
A pinch of salt
Extra chopped parsley and/or toasted pine-kernels to garnish

Make several fairly deep incisions in the aubergines with a sharp, pointed knife and insert the garlic slices into the flesh. Place them on a baking sheet and bake for about an hour at 180°C (350°F, Gas 4). (This can be done in advance while you are using the oven for something else.)

Allow to cool a little, then cut the aubergines in half and gently squeeze out any excess liquid (this will help remove the bitter juices). Scoop out the flesh and garlic slithers, discarding the skins, and mash or chop the flesh to a pulpy texture. Add the remaining ingredients and mix well. Season to taste, and serve with melba toast or hot arabic or pitta bread. You could also add a salad garnish and a sprinkling of chopped parsley or pine-kernels.

Note: If you are making this dish in advance, omit the pine-kernels and keep covered and chilled until needed, then fold in the pine-kernels just before serving.

Baked Jerusalem Artichoke Mould with Fines Herbes Sauce

Serves 6

12 oz (350g) Jerusalem artichokes
2 teaspoons lemon juice
12 oz (350g) firm tofu, crumbled
3 tablespoons oil
A pinch of nutmeg
$\frac{1}{2}$ bunch spring onions, finely chopped
Black pepper and salt
1–2 tablespoons fresh wholewheat *or* rye breadcrumbs
1 quantity fine herbes sauce (page 124)
Optional garnishes:
Watercress; chopped spring onion tops; 2–3 thin twists of lemon to garnish

Scrub, scrape or peel the Jerusalem artichokes to remove all the dark outer skin. Boil in a pan with the lemon juice and enough water to cover them until tender (about 10–12 minutes). Drain, allow to cool and then dice or roughly chop.

Meanwhile, preheat the oven to 180°C (350°F, Gas 4). Blend the tofu with the oil and nutmeg in a food processor or liquidizer until smooth. Fold in the spring onions and artichokes, and season to taste. Sprinkle the breadcrumbs onto the base and sides of a well greased 1$\frac{1}{2}$–2 pint (1–1.2 litres) soufflé or casserole dish. Spoon in the mixture, smooth the surface and bake in the centre of the oven for about 35 minutes, until the surface begins to brown.

Allow to cool in the dish for 5–10 minutes, then turn out and either cool completely or serve at once with a fines herbes sauce.

This dish is good served hot or cold. If serving cold, allow the fines herbes sauce to cool in a covered saucepan after making it, then beat well again before transferring to a serving dish or pouring over the artichoke mould.

Crispy Tofu Crunches with Tartare Sauce

Serves 6

**1 lb (450g) firm tofu *or*
  1 lb (450g) thawed
  and squeezed frozen
  tofu
4 tablespoons soy sauce
2 oz (50g) crispbread
  crumbs *or* wholemeal
  breadcrumbs
2 oz (50g) plain
  wholemeal flour
1 tablespoon dried
  parsley
1 teaspoon turmeric
2 teaspoons paprika
A good pinch (approx $\frac{1}{4}$
  teaspoon) of cayenne
  pepper
Black pepper and salt
2 tablespoons vegetable
  oil
1 quantity tartare sauce
  (see page 130)**

Cut the tofu into cubes or pieces about $\frac{1}{2}$–$\frac{3}{4}$ inch (1–2cm) in size. Marinate in the soy sauce for 1$\frac{1}{2}$–2 hours. Mix the bread or crispbread crumbs, flour, parsley and spices in a bowl or on a large plate. Season with black pepper and salt.

Preheat the oven to 200°C (400°F, Gas 6). Pour the oil into a small bowl and brush a baking sheet with some of it. Use the rest to coat each marinated tofu piece lightly before gently rolling it in the spiced crumb mixure, covering it as thickly as possible, and placing it on the oiled baking tray. Space the tofu pieces $\frac{1}{4}$–$\frac{1}{2}$ inch (5–10mm) apart on the tray and bake in the upper part of the oven for 15–20 minutes, then turn them over with a spatula and cook for a further 10–12 minutes.

Allow to cool slightly. Serve warm with a salad garnish and tartare sauce.

Stuffed Mushrooms

Serves 4

8 large, flat mushrooms
1 oz (25g) vegan margarine
1 dessertspoon olive oil
1-2 cloves garlic, crushed
1½ tablespoons sherry
1 rounded tablespoon fresh parsley, finely chopped
1 oz (25g) fresh wholewheat breadcrumbs
2 oz (50g) hard cheese (see page 35), grated
2-3 tablespoons vegetable stock *or* water
Black pepper
Extra parsley to garnish

Preheat the oven to 200°C (400°F, Gas 6). Carefully remove the stalks from the mushrooms and chop them finely. Heat the margarine and oil in a covered pan and cook the chopped stalks with the garlic for 8–10 minutes. Add the sherry and parsley and cook for a further minute. Remove from heat and allow to cool slightly, then stir in the breadcrumbs, cheese and enough of the stock or water to produce a moist but fairly firm consistency. Season to taste with black pepper. Spread the mixture over the fleshy side of the mushrooms and arrange them stuffed-side upwards in a lightly greased, shallow ovenproof dish. Cook in the oven for 15–20 minutes. Serve hot, garnished with parsley sprigs or a sprinkling of chopped parsley.

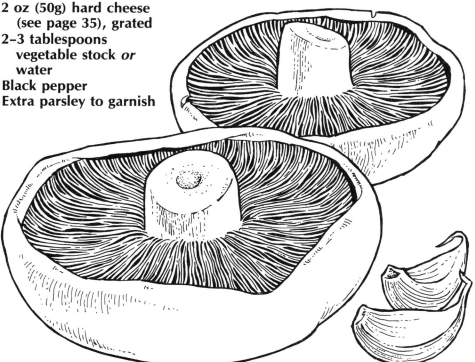

54

Vegan Vitality

Tofu in Watercress Mayonnaise

Serves 4

12 oz (350g) firm tofu, cut into ½-inch (1cm) cubes
½ teaspoon ground turmeric
6 oz (175g) silken tofu
2 oz (50g) watercress, rinsed, patted dry and roughly chopped
½ teaspoon prepared English mustard
1½ tablespoons sunflower oil
2 teaspoons freshly squeezed lemon juice
2 teaspoons cider vinegar
Freshly ground black pepper and salt
Extra watercress to garnish

Sprinkle the turmeric over the tofu and toss gently and briefly (the turmeric does not have to evenly colour the tofu — a variegated yellow/white appearance is actually preferable). Keep to one side on a serving dish or individual dishes. Place the remaining ingredients in a liquidizer and blend thoroughly.

Pour the mayonnaise over the tofu and serve, garnished with extra watercress if desired.

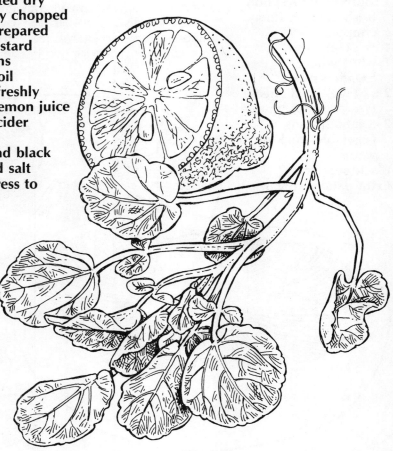

Avocado and Pear Hollandaise

Serves 4-6

2 large, ripe avocados
2 large dessert pears
1 tablespoon lemon
 juice
1 quantity cold
 Hollandaise sauce
 (see page 130)
Lettuce leaves and a
 little chopped, fresh
 tarragon *or* chives to
 garnish

Peel the avocados and pears one at a time. Cut each in half after peeling, then cut each half into 4 wedges along its length. Coat the pieces in lemon juice to prevent discolouration, then proceed in the same way with the remaining fruits. Make a bed of lettuce on each serving plate and arrange the wedges, using avocado and dessert pear alternately, to make a fan-shape on the lettuce. Spoon or carefully pour over the Hollandaise sauce (a broad, slanting zig-zag pattern looks attractive), and garnish with a sprinkling of chopped, fresh tarragon or chives.

Note: For a simple refreshing salad which is a variation on this two-pear theme, and which can also be served as a starter, see Avocado, Pear and Olive Salad (page 117).

Spiced Lentil and Coconut Pâté

Serves 6-8

8 oz (225g) red lentils
1 small/medium red
 pepper, finely
 chopped
1 tablespoon oil
2 level teaspoons curry
 powder
1 pint (575ml) water
2 oz (50g) creamed
 coconut, grated
2 tablespoons peanut
 butter
A squeeze of lemon
 juice
5-6 fl oz (150-175ml)
 soya yoghurt
Lightly toasted,
 dessicated coconut to
 garnish

Pick the lentils over to remove any stones, or grit and rinse thoroughly. Sauté the red pepper in the oil with the curry powder for 4-5 minutes. Stir in the lentils and water, bring to the boil and simmer for about 20 minutes until soft. Add the creamed coconut, stirring over a low heat until dissolved. Remove from the heat and mix in the peanut butter and lemon juice, beating thoroughly until a smooth purée is obtained. Allow to cool, then chill the mixture for at least 1 hour. Mix in the soya yoghurt and divide the pâté between individual ramekin dishes. Sprinkle a little toasted, dessicated coconut over each portion and serve with warm pitta bread, wholemeal rolls or melba toast.

Tangy Spinach and Cream Cheese Pâté

Serves 4

8 oz (225g) cream cheese (see page 36)
½ oz (12g) vegan soft margarine
4 oz (100g) blanched or frozen, thawed spinach
4 tablespoons freshly squeezed orange juice
Finely grated rind of half an orange
2 teaspoons concentrated orange juice
A good pinch each of paprika and nutmeg
A dash of tabasco sauce
Black pepper and salt
4 thin twists of orange to garnish

Beat the cheese and margarine together until light and fluffy. Squeeze out as much excess moisture as possible from the blanched or thawed spinach, then chop finely. Fold into the cheese mixture. Add the freshly-squeezed orange juice a tablespoon at a time, beating well after each addition to ensure that a light, smooth texture is kept. Finally, beat in the orange rind, concentrated orange juice, spices and tabasco sauce. Season to taste and divide between 4 ramekin dishes. Chill in the refrigerator for at least 2 hours, then garnish each portion with a twist of orange and serve with warm melba toast.

Guacamole

Serves 4–6

2 large, ripe avocados
1 tablespoon grated
onion
1 clove garlic, crushed
1 tablespoon freshly
squeezed lemon juice
1 tomato, skinned,
seeded and finely
chopped
A pinch of chilli
powder
1 dessertspoon olive oil
3 tablespoons soya
yoghurt
A pinch of salt
Twists of cucumber to
garnish

Scoop out the flesh from the avocados and mash it with the onion, garlic and lemon juice. Add the tomato, chilli powder and oil and beat to obtain a purée-like consistency. Fold in the soya yoghurt until evently blended, and season to taste with a little salt. Transfer the mixture to a serving dish or divide between individual ramekins, then cover and chill for at least an hour before serving.

Garnish with twists (thin slices twisted into an 'S' shape) of cucumber and serve with melba toast or crispy tortillas (see note on page 178).

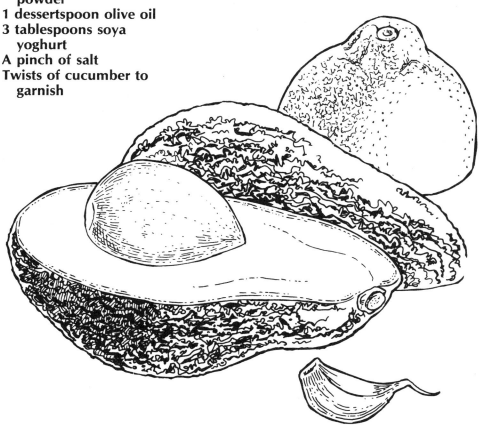

Mushroom, Onion and Nut Pâté

Serves 6–8

2 oz (50g) brazil nuts
2 oz (50g) cashew nut
   pieces
2 oz (50g) walnut
   pieces
2 oz (50g) peanuts
   (rinsed and patted
   dry if salted)
1 oz (25g) vegan
   margarine
1 tablespoon oil
1 large onion, finely
   chopped
1 clove garlic, crushed
   (optional)
6 oz (175g) mushrooms,
   wiped and finely
   chopped
1 teaspoon dried mixed
   herbs
1 heaped teaspoon
   miso
2 tablespoons soy sauce
1 tablespoon sherry
$\frac{1}{4}$ pint (150ml) water
2 oz (50g) fresh,
   wholemeal
   breadcrumbs
1 tablespoon soya flour
1 tablespoon arrowroot
Black pepper and salt
4 walnut halves to
   garnish

Preheat the oven to 180°C (350°F, Gas 4). Mix the nuts together and grind, or finely crush or chop. Heat the margarine and oil in a saucepan and cook the onion, garlic, mushrooms and herbs, covered, for 7–8 minutes. Stir in the miso until evenly blended, then add the soy sauce, sherry and water. Heat to a simmer and cook uncovered for 4–5 minutes. Remove from heat and stir in the nuts and breadcrumbs. Mix the soya flour and arrowroot to a thin paste with a little water and blend well with the other ingredients. Season with a little salt and freshly ground black pepper and spoon the mixture into a well-greased 1 lb (500g) loaf tin. Bake in the centre of the oven for 35–40 minutes. Remove and allow to cool completely before turning out of the tin.

This can be made one or two days in advance and kept in the refrigerator, if required.

Garnish with a line of about 4 walnut halves down the centre. If you want an extra decorative finish, flank the walnut halves with whole cashew-nut crescents or slices of button mushroom.

MAIN COURSES

Tofu dishes

Barbecued Tofu

Serves 4–6

1½ lb (675g) firm frozen
  tofu, thawed
3 tablespoons sunflower
  or safflower oil
3 tablespoons peanut
  butter
3 tablespoons tomato
  juice
1 teaspoon paprika
½ teaspoon chilli
  powder
Black pepper and salt
1 quantity barbecue
  sauce (see page 129)

Gently squeeze out any excess liquid from the thawed tofu to leave a spongy, absorbent texture. Cut it into strips. Whisk together the oil, peanut butter, tomato juice, spices and seasoning. Pour over the tofu pieces, coating them as evenly as possible, and leave to marinate for at least 2 hours. Preheat the oven to 190°C (375°F, Gas 5). Arrange the tofu pieces on a well-oiled baking sheet or shallow, flat-bottomed ovenproof dish, brush them with a little extra oil and bake in the upper part of the oven for 20–25 minutes.

Serve with the heated barbecue sauce, hot garlic bread and a crisp side salad.

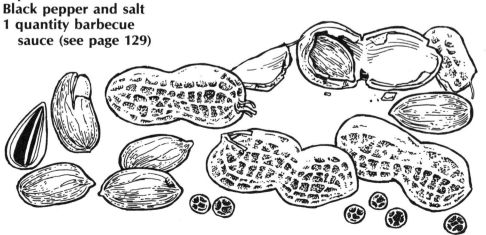

Broccoli Tofu Soufflé

Serves 4–6

8 oz (225g) broccoli
1 oz (25g) vegan
  margarine
1 medium onion, finely
  chopped
½ teaspoon dried
  marjoram
1 teaspoon paprika
½ teaspoon cayenne
  pepper
1½ oz (37g) fine-milled,
  wholemeal flour
1 dessertspoon soya
  flour
6 fl oz (175ml) soya
  milk
2 fl oz (50ml) apple
  juice
A pinch of nutmeg
Black pepper and salt
8 oz (225g) firm tofu
2 tablespoons sunflower
  oil
Juice of half a lemon
1 level teaspoon
  mustard powder
½ teaspoon baking
  powder

Preheat the oven to 180°C (350°F, Gas 4). Place the broccoli in a pan with a little water and blanch for 5–7 minutes. Allow to cool, then drain and chop fairly finely.

Melt the margarine in a medium saucepan and fry the onion with the marjoram, paprika and cayenne for 4–5 minutes until softened. Add the flours and stir with a wooden spoon to make a roux. Remove from heat and gradually add the soya milk and apple juice, stirring all the time to keep the consistency smooth. Season with the nutmeg, black pepper and salt to taste, then fold in the chopped broccoli and keep to one side.

Blend the tofu with the oil, lemon juice, mustard powder and baking powder in a liquidizer or food processor until creamy. Add this to the broccoli mixture and fold in thoroughly and evenly. Adjust seasoning if required, then transfer to a lightly greased 2-pint (1 litre) soufflé or other suitable ovenproof dish and bake for 35–40 minutes in the oven, until top is slightly browned.

This dish can be served as a starter or a main course, by itself, or with a sauce such as tomato and cheese, rich tomato (page 127), or mushroom cream (page 125).

It also goes well with baked potatoes and steamed or ginger-glazed carrots (page 135).

Singapore Kebabs

Serves 4

1½ lb (675g) frozen
  tofu, thawed
1 tablespoon cumin
  seeds
2 tablespoons coriander
  seeds
2 tablespoons oil
2 teaspoons ground
  aniseed
½ teaspoon ground
  turmeric
1 walnut-sized piece of
  fresh ginger root,
  grated
1 medium onion, grated
  or very finely
  chopped
3 oz (75g) creamed
  coconut, grated
½ pint (275ml) hot
  water
Extra oil for brushing

Peanut Sauce:
1 small onion, chopped
1 clove garlic, crushed
1 tablespoon oil
4 oz (100g) peanuts,
  ground, *or* 4 oz
  (100g) peanut butter
½ pint (275ml) hot
  water
1 tablespoon tamari

Squeeze out the excess liquid from the thawed tofu. Cut into kebab-size pieces or cubes, and keep to one side.

Grind the seeds in a grinder and fry them in the heated oil with the aniseed, turmeric and ginger for about 2 minutes, stirring frequently and taking care not to burn the mixture. Add the onion and cook for a further minute. Remove from the heat. Put the creamed coconut and hot water in a liquidizer and blend until dissolved. Gradually add this to the saucepan, stirring all the time. Pour this mixture over the tofu pieces and leave to marinate for 2–3 hours. After this time, thread the marinated tofu onto kebab skewers and arrange in an oiled, shallow, ovenproof dish. Preheat the oven to 190°C (375°F, Gas 5). Brush with a little extra oil mixed with any remaining marinade and bake in the oven for 25–30 minutes.

To prepare the sauce, fry the onion and garlic in the oil for 4–5 minutes over a low/medium heat. Stir in the ground peanuts or peanut butter, then gradually add the mixed hot water and tamari, stirring all the time to keep the consistency smooth and even. Either serve separately in a warmed jug or tureen, or pour over the cooked kebabs.

This dish is superb with freshly cooked brown rice and a light side salad of thin sticks of cucumber, celery and mooli or red pepper.

Orange and Sesame Sautéed Tofu

Serves 4

1 lb (450g) firm tofu

Marinade:
**1 tablespoon light
  tahini**
**1 tablespoon sunflower
  or safflower oil**
2 tablespoons shoyu
**Juice and finely grated
  rind of half an
  orange**
Black pepper
1 oz (25g) sesame seeds

Sauce:
**Any remaining
  marinade**
Juice of half an orange
**2 tablespoons light
  tahini**
3 fl oz (75ml) water
**3 fl oz (75ml) apple
  juice**
$\frac{1}{2}$ tablespoon soy sauce
**Blanched strands of
  orange rind or extra
  sesame seeds to
  garnish**

Cut the tofu into oblong strips or pieces (about $1 \times 2 \times \frac{1}{2}$ inches, or $2.5 \times 5 \times 1$cm). Whisk the marinade ingredients together and coat the tofu pieces in it. Leave to marinate for $2-2\frac{1}{2}$ hours, then cook the pieces in a heated, dry frying pan over a moderate heat for 5–7 minutes on each side.

Meanwhile, combine any remaining marinade with the sauce ingredients and heat in a small saucepan, stirring frequently.

When the tofu pieces are cooked, transfer them to a warmed serving dish, pour over the sauce and garnish with blanched strands of orange rind, or a sprinkling of sesame seeds.

This is good with freshly cooked rice or tofu noodles (see page 94).

Savoury Tofu Loaf

Serves 6–8

1 medium/large onion,
  chopped
1 clove garlic (optional)
2 tablespoons vegetable
  oil
3 sticks celery, chopped
1 lb (450g) tofu,
  mashed
4 oz (100g) oatmeal *or*
  rolled oats
3 tomatoes, washed
  and chopped
3 tablespoons soy sauce
3 tablespoons tomato
  purée
A dash of tabasco, *or* $\frac{1}{4}$
  teaspoon cayenne
  pepper
1 teaspoon dry mustard
  powder
1 teaspoon chopped
  basil
2 tablespoons fresh
  parsley, finely
  chopped
Black pepper and salt
Tomato slices and
  sprigs of parsley to
  garnish

(This mixture can also be used to make tofu burgers. Simply roll in oatmeal or breadcrumbs and shallow fry or grill.)

Preheat the oven to 180°C (350°F, Gas 4). Sauté the onion and garlic (if using) in the oil for about 5 minutes until soft but not browned. Add the celery and sauté gently for a further 5–7 minutes. Remove from the heat, add the remaining ingredients and mix thoroughly. Press the mixture into a greased 2 lb (1kg) loaf tin, cover the top with foil and bake for 60–65 minutes.

Leave for about 5 minutes after removing from the oven before turning onto a warmed serving dish.

Garnish with slices of tomato and a few sprigs of parsley. Serve with tomato or barbeque sauce, roast or baked potatoes and a steamed vegetable.

Javanese Sunflower Tofu

Serves 4

1 lb (450g) firm tofu
1 tablespoon sunflower
**   spread**
1 tablespoon peanut
**   butter**
1 clove garlic, crushed
1 tablespoon sunflower
**   oil**
A pinch of ground bay
**   leaves**
1 dessertspoon freshly
**   squeezed lemon juice**
3 tablespoons soy sauce
A dash of tabasco sauce
**   *or* a small pinch of**
**   chilli powder**
1 teaspoon fresh, grated
**   root ginger**
4 tablespoons hot water
**   *or* 4 tablespoons**
**   pineapple juice**
Black pepper and salt
1 tablespoon sunflower
**   seeds *or* chopped**
**   peanuts**

Cut the tofu into rectangular slices approximately 2×1 inches (5×2.5cm) and about ½ inch (1cm) thick. Blend together the rest of the ingredients *except* the sunflower seeds or chopped peanuts. Whisk to make a sauce and pour half of the mixture onto the base of a shallow square or rectangular ovenproof dish (approximately 9×12 inches, or 22×30cm). Arrange the tofu slices over this, then pour over the remaining sauce. Marinate for 1½–2 hours, then sprinkle the sunflower seeds or chopped peanuts (or a mixture of these) over the dish. Preheat the oven to 180°C (350°F, Gas 4). Bake for 25–30 minutes.

Serve hot with freshly cooked brown rice and lightly steamed or stir-fried vegetables.

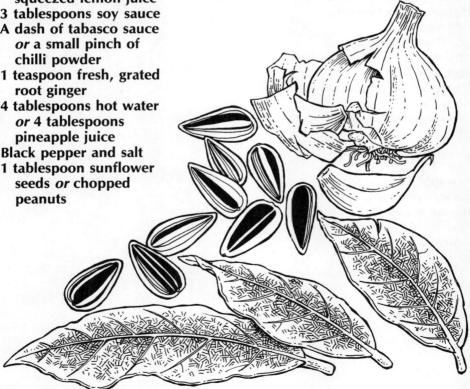

Tofu Foo Yong

Serves 4

1 oz (25g) vegan
  margarine
4 oz (100g) mushrooms,
  chopped
1 teaspoon miso
1 bunch spring onions,
  chopped
4 oz (100g) mange-
  touts, diagonally
  sliced
1 lb (450g) firm tofu,
  crumbled
3 tablespoons shoyu
1 oz (25g) wholemeal
  flour
½ oz (12g) soya flour
1 level teaspoon baking
  powder
Black pepper and salt
A few chopped spring
  onion tops to garnish

Sweet and Sour Sauce:
2 oz (50g) mushrooms,
  finely chopped
1 tablespoon sunflower
  oil
1 tablespoon chopped
  spring onions
  (reserved from Foo
  Yong ingredients)
½ pint (275ml) water
1½ tablespoons shoyu
2 teaspoons cider
  vinegar
2 teaspoons brown
  sugar
2 level teaspoons
  cornflour

Preheat the oven to 180°C (350°C, Gas 4). Melt the margarine in a wok or saucepan and sauté the mushrooms for 3–4 minutes. Stir in the miso until dissolved or evenly blended. Reserve a tablespoon of the chopped spring onions for the sauce, then add the rest to the mushrooms with the mange-touts, and cook for a further minute or two. Cover and remove from heat. Blend the tofu with the shoyu in a food processor or liquidizer, or with an electric hand-whisk, until it is smooth and creamy. Sift the flours together with the baking powder and fold into the tofu. Season sparingly with black pepper and salt. Combine the vegetables with the tofu mixture and mix gently. Use an ice-cream scoop, if you have one, to scoop out even quantities of the mixture and deposit these on well greased baking sheets about 1 inch (2.5cm) apart. Flatten the mounds slightly with the back of the scoop and bake for 20–25 minutes, until expanded and lightly browned. Then flip over with a spatula and bake for a further 8–12 minutes.

Meanwhile, prepare the sauce. Cook the mushrooms in the oil for 5–7 minutes in a covered pan. Add the spring onions and cook for another minute. Stir in the water, shoyu, vinegar and sugar. Bring to the boil, stirring occasionally, and simmer on a low heat for 8–10 minutes. Mix the cornflour to a thin paste with a little cold water and briskly stir this into the sauce until it thickens.

Arrange the baked rounds on a serving plate, pour over the sauce and sprinkle on any reserved spring onion tops to garnish.

Serve immediately with freshly cooked tofu noodles (see page 94).

Pulse dishes

Chilli Con Coconut

Serves 4

**6 oz (175g) red kidney
  beans**
**2 tablespoons vegetable
  oil**
1 large onion
1 clove garlic
**1 teaspoon dried
  marjoram**
1 teaspoon cumin
**$\frac{1}{2}$ teaspoon chilli
· powder**
1 yellow pepper, diced
**4 oz (100g) sweetcorn
  kernels**
**1 × 14 oz (400g) tin
  tomatoes, roughly
  ·chopped**
**2 tablespoons tomato
  purée**
**1 oz (25g) creamed
  coconut, grated**
**$\frac{1}{4}$–$\frac{1}{2}$ pint (150–275ml)
  kidney bean stock**
**1 tablespoon freshly
  squeezed lemon juice**
Black pepper and salt
**Toasted, dessicated or
  shredded coconut to
  garnish**

Soak the beans overnight or hot soak (see page 183). Rinse the soaked beans well and put in a medium saucepan with 1$\frac{1}{2}$ pints (850ml) fresh water. Bring to the boil, cover and simmer for abour 45 minutes until just becoming tender.

Meanwhile, heat the oil in a large saucepan and sauté the onion and garlic together with the marjoram and spices for 5–6 minutes. Add the diced pepper and cook for a further 2–3 minutes. Stir in the sweetcorn kernels, tomatoes, tomato purée and creamed coconut. Bring gently to the boil, stirring constantly to make sure that the coconut dissolves completely. Add the cooked beans with $\frac{1}{4}$ pint (150ml) of their stock and simmer for 25–30 minutes, checking occasionally to add more stock if a thinner consistency is desired. Stir in the lemon juice, season to taste, transfer to a warmed serving dish and garnish with a light sprinkling of toasted coconut. Serve hot with tortillas (see page 178), and a side salad.

Pinto Bean Goulash with Soured Cream

Serves 4

4 oz (100g) pinto beans
2 oz (50g) wheat grain
1 medium aubergine, diced into pieces of $\frac{1}{2}$-$\frac{3}{4}$ inch (1–2cm)
2 tablespoons oil
1 large onion, chopped
1 clove garlic, chopped
1 teaspoon paprika
$\frac{1}{4}$ teaspoon cayenne pepper
1 green pepper, diced
8 oz (225g) tomatoes, skinned and chopped
1 teaspoon dried basil (*or* 2 teaspoons chopped, fresh basil)
$\frac{1}{2}$ teaspoon caraway seeds
$\frac{1}{2}$ pint (275ml) tomato juice
$\frac{1}{2}$ pint (275ml) stock from beans and wheat grain
1 bay leaf
2 tablespoons shoyu
A squeeze of lemon juice
2 tablespoons chopped, fresh parsley
Black pepper and salt
1 quantity tofu soured cream (page 34)

Soak the pinto beans and wheat grain overnight or hot soak (see page 183). Drain, rinse well and bring to the boil in $1\frac{1}{4}$ pints (725ml) fresh water. Simmer for about 1 hour until tender.

Meanwhile, place the thickly diced aubergine in a colander and sprinkle liberally with salt. Leave to stand for 30 minutes, then rinse thoroughly under a cold tap to remove salt and bitter juices. Pat dry on kitchen paper. Heat oil in a large covered saucepan and sauté the onion and garlic with the prepared aubergine, paprika and cayenne for 5–6 minutes. Stir in the green pepper, chopped tomatoes, basil and caraway seeds and cook for a further 2–3 minutes. Add the tomato juice, the cooked beans and wheat grain with $\frac{1}{2}$ pint (275ml) of their stock, the bay leaf and shoyu. Simmer gently, uncovered, for 25–30 minutes until flavours are well blended and liquid has reduced to a thickened consistency. Stir in the lemon juice and parsley, keeping a little aside for garnish if desired, season to taste and transfer to a warmed serving dish. Spoon over the soured cream to form an attractive zig-zag or swirl pattern on top of the goulash, and sprinkle over any reserved parsley. Serve hot with steamed or jacket potatoes and a steamed green vegetable such as green beans or broccoli.

Note: Soya yoghurt is a slightly lighter alternative to soured cream.

Aduki Bean Tacos

Serves 6

**8 oz (225ml) aduki
 beans**
1 bay leaf
**2 tablespoons vegetable
 oil**
1 large onion, chopped
**2 medium carrots
 (about 4 oz or 100g),
 grated**
**1 red pepper, finely
 diced**
**1 fresh green or red
 chilli, finely chopped**
**1½ teaspoons dried
 marjoram**
**1 teaspoon ground
 cumin**
**2 heaped teaspoons
 miso**
**3 tablespoons tomato
 purée**
Black pepper and salt
**Freshly cooked tortillas
 to serve (see page
 178)**

Soak the aduki beans overnight or hot soak (see page 183). Drain, rinse well and bring to the boil with the bay leaf in 1¼ pints (725ml) fresh water. Reduce heat, cover and simmer for about 1 hour until soft. Mash roughly with any remaining liquid and keep to one side.

Heat the oil in a large saucepan and fry the onion for 2–3 minutes until softened. Stir in the carrots, red pepper, chilli, marjoram and cumin. Continue to cook, covered, for a further 3–4 minutes over a low heat. Remove from heat and mix in the miso, tomato purée, and mashed beans. Heat the mixture to a simmer and cook uncovered, stirring frequently, for 10–15 minutes, or until it has become thick enough to spoon into the warm tortillas. Season to taste and serve with the tortillas and a crisp salad.

Lentil Moussaka

Serves 4–6

- **4 oz (100g) continental lentils**
- **2 oz (50g) green lentils**
- **2 medium aubergines**
- **3 tablespoons vegetable oil**
- **1 medium/large onion, chopped**
- **1–2 cloves garlic, crushed**
- **4 oz (100g) mushrooms, wiped and sliced**
- **1 teaspoon dried marjoram**
- **½ pint (275ml) stock from cooked lentils**
- **1 × 14 oz (400g) tin tomatoes**
- **3 tablespoons red wine (optional)**
- **2 tablespoons soy sauce**
- **1 tablespoon tomato purée**
- **1 fresh or dried bouquet garni**
- **1 tablespoon fresh parsley, finely chopped**
- **Black pepper and salt**
- **1 quantity bechamel sauce (see page 123)**
- **A good pinch of nutmeg**
- **2 oz (50g) vegan hard cheese (see page 35), grated**
- **A little paprika for dusting**

Remove any stones or grit from the lentils and rinse them thoroughly in a sieve. Place in a medium saucepan with 1 pint (575ml) water and bring to the boil. Simmer for about 40 minutes until soft. Trim and wash the aubergines and slice them into ¼-inch (5mm) thick circles. Sprinkle liberally with salt and leave to stand for at least 30 minutes, then rinse thoroughly and pat dry on kitchen paper.

While waiting for the lentils and aubergines, heat 1 tablespoon of the oil in a large covered saucepan and cook the onion, garlic, mushrooms and marjoram for 10 minutes over a low heat. Add the cooked lentils with ½ pint (275ml) of their stock, the tomatoes (breaking these up a little as you stir them in), red wine if using, soy sauce, tomato purée and bouquet garni. Bring gently to the boil and simmer uncovered for 15–20 minutes, adding the parsley for the last 5 minutes of cooking time. Season to taste and keep to one side. Next, heat a little of the remaining oil in a large frying pan and cook the aubergine slices in batches for 3–4 minutes on each side over a moderate heat, adding a little more of the oil for each batch (try not to use extra oil or the finished dish will taste greasy).

Preheat the oven to 180°C (350°F, Gas 4). Lightly grease a 3-pint (2 litre) ovenproof dish and spoon in half the lentil mixture. Cover this with a layer of aubergine slices (reserving the more evenly-sized slices for the top layer). Repeat the layers, finishing with an arrangement of overlapping aubergine rings around the edge of the dish.

Pour the bechamel sauce evenly over the top surface of the dish, then sprinkle with the grated cheese and dust with a little paprika to give the cooked dish a deeper golden appearance. Bake for 35–40 minutes.

Serve with a crisp salad and hot, crusty bread.

Mixed Bean Hotpot with Sage Dumplings

Serves 4–6

2 oz (50g) red kidney
  beans
2 oz (50g) haricot beans
2 oz (50g) flageolet
  beans
2 tablespoons vegetable
  oil
6 oz (175g) whole
  pickling onions
3 oz (75g) mushrooms
½ teaspoon dried
  rosemary
1 teaspoon dried thyme
6 oz (175g) swede,
  diced
6 oz (175g) parsnips
  (about 2 medium),
  diced
½ teaspoon celery seed
½ pint (275ml) stock
  from cooked beans
8 oz (225g) tomatoes,
  skinned and chopped
1 tablespoon tomato
  purée
3 tablespoons tamari
4 fl oz (100ml) red wine
1 oz (25g) pot barley
6 oz (175g) Brussels
  sprouts, *or* fine green
  beans, cut into ¾-inch
  (2–2.5cm) lengths
Black pepper and salt

Soak the beans overnight or hot soak (see page 183). Bring to the boil in 1½ pints (1 litre) water, then reduce heat and simmer for 40–50 minutes until just becoming tender. Drain and reserve the stock.

Heat the oil in a large covered saucepan and gently sauté the onions, mushrooms and herbs for 5–7 minutes. Add the swede, parsnip and celery seed and continue to cook for a further 3–4 minutes. Stir in ½ pint (275ml) of stock from the beans together with the beans, tomatoes, tomato purée, tamari, red wine and pot barley. Bring to the boil and simmer for 10–15 minutes, stirring occasionally.

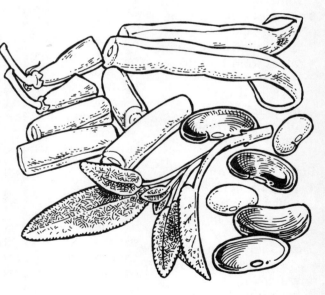

Dumplings:
3 oz (75g) fine-milled, wholemeal self-raising flour
1 oz (25g) barley flour
¼ teaspoon baking powder
A pinch of salt
1 level teaspoon dried, rubbed sage, *or 2* teaspoons chopped, fresh sage
1½ oz (37g) grated Suenut
4–5 tablespoons cold water

Meanwhile, prepare the dumplings. Sift the flours and baking powder together into a mixing bowl and stir in the salt, sage and suenut. Add enough of the cold water to make a soft dough. Knead lightly for a minute or two in the bowl, then shape into 8 balls.

Stir the brussel sprouts or green beans into the hotpot, season to taste, then arrange the dumplings on the top. Cover and keep the casserole simmering on a low heat, without removing the lid, for 20–25 minutes, until the dumplings have expanded and are light and fluffy.

Serve at once.

Arabian Hummus

Serves 6–8

8 oz (225g) chick peas, soaked overnight
1½ pints (850ml) water
2–3 cloves garlic, crushed
Juice of 1 lemon
5 oz (150g) (about 4 rounded tablespoons) light tahini
3 fl oz (75ml) olive oil
Black pepper and salt

Topping:
2 oz (50g) soya mince (preferably dark-coloured for contrast)
¼ pint (150ml) water
2 tablespoons soy sauce
1 tablespoon pine-kernels

Drain and rinse the soaked chick peas thoroughly. Place in a pan with the water, bring to the boil and simmer for 1¼–1½ hours until tender. Drain and reserve the stock.

Preheat the oven to 150°C (300°F, Gas 2). Blend the chick peas together with ¼ pint (150ml) of their stock and all the other ingredients in a food processor or liquidizer, adding more stock if necessary to achieve a smooth, moist, creamy consistency. This can be eaten cold with or without the topping, but if trying the warmed version, transfer the hummus to a 2-pint (1 litre) ovenproof dish (preferably round or oval), building up the edges to form a shallow well in the centre. Cover with foil and place in the oven for about 10 minutes. Meanwhile, prepare the topping.

Place the soya mince in a small pan with the water and soy sauce and simmer for 10–12 minutes until most of the water (but not all) has been absorbed. Take the hummus out of the oven and fluff the edges over with a fork to remove any slightly 'baked' look on the surface. Pour the soya mince mixture into the centre well and garnish with a sprinkling of pine nuts. Serve immediately with hot arabic or pitta bread.

Black-eye Biriani

Serves 4

4 oz (100g) black-eyed
  beans
2 dessertspoons oil
1 large onion, chopped
1 clove garlic, crushed
1 teaspoon garam
  masala
1 teaspoon mustard
  seeds
2 teaspoons ground
  coriander
1 teaspoon turmeric
1 teaspoon cumin seeds
1 teaspoon cardamon
  seeds
½ teaspoon chilli
  powder
½ medium cauliflower,
  cut into small florets
8 oz (225g) okra,
  trimmed, washed and
  sliced
1 green or red pepper,
  cored, seeded,
  washed and diced
2 tablespoons tomato
  purée
1 tablespoon peanut
  butter
½ pint (275ml) black-
  eyed bean stock
12 oz (350g) tomatoes,
  washed and chopped
1 dessertspoon lemon
  juice
Black pepper and salt

Soak beans overnight or hot soak (see page 183). Drain, rinse well and bring to boil in 1½ pints (850ml) fresh water. Simmer for about 35 minutes until just tender. Drain and reserve stock.

Meanwhile, heat the oil in a large saucepan and sauté the onion, garlic, spices and seeds for 7–8 minutes over a low/medium heat until softened and golden in colour. Stir in the cauliflower florets, okra and green or red pepper and sauté for a further 2–3 minutes. Dissolve the tomato purée and peanut butter in the warm stock. Add this to the pan along with the tomatoes and black-eyed beans, and simmer for 15–20 minutes.

Add the lemon juice, season to taste and serve on a bed of freshly cooked brown rice, preferably with a side salad of diced cucumber mixed with soya yoghurt and a little chopped, fresh mint.

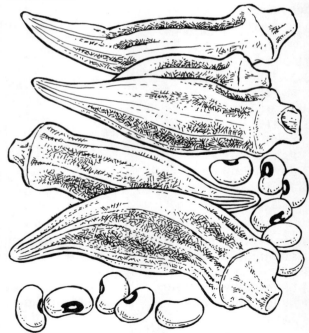

Nut dishes

Broccoli and Chestnut Bake

Serves 4

6 oz (175g) chestnuts
1–1¼ pints (575–725ml) soya milk
1 level teaspoon cut, dried bay leaves
1 lb (450g) potatoes, peeled or well scrubbed
2 oz (50g) vegan margarine
1 tablespoon concentrated soya milk
Black pepper and salt
1 medium-large onion, sliced into rings
1 tablespoon oil
10 oz (275g) broccoli florets
6 oz (175g) button mushrooms, wiped and thinly sliced
1 oz (25g) plain, fine-milled, wholemeal flour
A pinch of nutmeg

Place the chestnuts in a bowl with 1 pint (575ml) soya milk and the bay leaves. Leave to soak for at least 2 hours, or overnight. Transfer to a saucepan, heat to boiling and simmer, covered, over a very low heat for 25–30 minutes, stirring occasionally.

Meanwhile, boil the potatoes until tender, drain and mash with ½ oz (12g) of the margarine and the concentrated soya milk until creamy. Season to taste, cover and set aside.

In a separate pan, sauté the onion rings in the heated oil for a few minutes until soft, then add the broccoli, cover and cook gently for a further 5–7 minutes. Remove from heat. Drain the milk from the cooked chestnuts into a measuring jug and make up to ¾ pint (425ml) if necessary. Add the chestnuts to the onion and broccoli and replace lid.

Preheat the oven to 180°C (350°F, Gas 4). Melt the remaining margarine in the pan which was used for simmering the chestnuts and cook the mushrooms, covered, for 8–10 minutes. Add the flour and stir with a wooden spoon to make a roux. Gradually add the reserved milk (from the chestnuts), stirring all the time to ensure an even consistency. When all the milk has been added, increase the heat and continue to stir until the sauce thickens. Add a pinch of nutmeg and season with black pepper and salt if desired.

Lightly oil a 3–4 pint (2–2.5 litre) casserole dish, and spoon in the broccoli, chestnut and onion mixture. Pour the mushroom sauce over this and top with the mashed potato. Fluff up the surface with a fork and bake for 30–40 minutes, until the potato topping is lightly browned.

Almond and Mushroom Stroganoff

Serves 3–4

1 tablespoon vegetable oil

4 oz (100g) split or flaked almonds

1 medium onion, sliced thinly into rings

$\frac{1}{2}$ oz (12g) vegan margarine

6 oz (175g) mushrooms, wiped and sliced

1 teaspoon ground coriander

$\frac{1}{2}$ teaspoon ground cinnamon

1 teaspoon dried tarragon

$\frac{1}{2}$ teaspoon ground or cut, dried bay leaves

4 sticks celery, *or* $\frac{1}{2}$ small bulb fennel, cut into thin strips

3 oz (75g) beanshoots

1 red pepper, cut into strips

2 tablespoons soy sauce

1 tablespoon sherry (optional)

5 tablespoons concentrated soya milk

Black pepper and salt

Toasted flaked almonds, *or* rings of red pepper, *or* extra concentrated soya milk to garnish

Heat the oil in a large saucepan, add the sliced onion and almonds, and sauté, stirring occasionally, for 3–4 minutes until the onion is transparent and the almonds slightly toasted. Add the margarine. When it has melted, add the mushrooms, spices and herbs. Stir in and reduce the heat a little. Cover the pan and simmer for a further 5–7 minutes. Then add the celery or fennel, beanshoots, red pepper, soy sauce and sherry if using. Cover and continue to simmer on a low heat for 10 minutes. When vegetables are just tender add the soya milk and stir in gently to heat (do not boil). Season to taste, transfer to a warmed serving dish and garnish with toasted, flaked almonds or with 2 or 3 rings of red pepper, or simply with a swirl of extra concentrated soya milk.

Stroganoff is superb served with jacket potatoes, or wholewheat tofu noodles (page 94), or on a bed of freshly cooked brown rice.

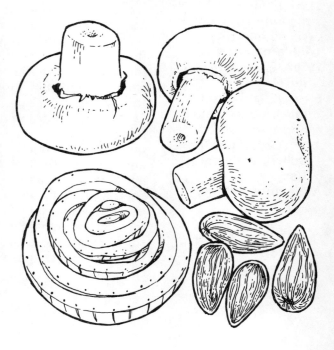

Courgette and Cashew Nut Crisp

Serves 4

4 oz (100g) mushrooms, wiped and sliced
3 oz (75g) vegan margarine
4 oz (100g) cashew nuts (whole if possible)
$\frac{1}{2}$ teaspoon dried tarragon, *or* 1 teaspoon fresh, chopped tarragon
1 lb (450g) courgettes, trimmed, washed and sliced into $\frac{1}{4}$-inch (5mm) rings
1 tablespoon wholemeal flour
1 rounded teaspoon soya flour
$\frac{1}{2}$ pint (275ml) soya milk
Juice and finely grated rind of half a lemon
$3\frac{1}{2}$ oz (87g) wholemeal breadcrumbs
1 tablespoon fresh parsley, finely chopped
Black pepper and salt

Melt 1 oz (25g) of the margarine in a pan and sauté half the mushrooms with the cashew nuts and tarragon for 5–7 minutes. Add the courgettes and continue cooking for a further 10–12 minutes.

Meanwhile, melt a further 1 oz (25g) of margarine in another pan and sauté the remaining mushrooms for about 5 minutes. Add the flours and beat to a roux with a wooden spoon. Gradually add the milk, stirring constantly, then increase the heat a little and stir until the sauce has thickened. Reduce the heat again and add the lemon juice a little at a time, still stirring, to prevent curdling. Season to taste, remove from heat and cover. Finally, melt the remaining 1 oz (25g) margarine and add the breadcrumbs. Keep tossing over a medium heat until crisp, taking care not to burn the mixture. Stir in the lemon rind and parsley.

To serve, place the courgette and cashew mixture on a warmed serving dish, pour over the mushroom and lemon sauce and top with the crsipy breadcrumb mixture.

This dish is excellent with jacket potatoes, or with freshly cooked brown rice.

Cashew and Walnut Roast

Serves 6–8

1½ oz (37g) vegan
  margarine
3–4 oz (75–100g)
  mushrooms, chopped
1 medium/large onion,
  finely chopped
1 small tin of tomatoes
1 rounded teaspoon
  yeast extract
2 tablespoons tomato
  purée
1 teaspoon fresh
  chopped marjoram *or*
  ½ teaspoon dried
  marjoram
1 teaspoon fresh,
  chopped basil *or* ½
  teaspoon dried basil
1 tablespoon fresh,
  chopped parsley
4 oz (100g) walnuts,
  ground
4 oz (100g) cashew
  nuts, ground
3 oz (75g) fresh
  wholemeal
  breadcrumbs
1 heaped tablespoon
  wheatgerm
Black pepper and salt
1 tablespoon soya flour
1 tablespoon arrowroot

Preheat the oven to 180°C (350°F, Gas 4). Melt the margarine in a large frying pan or saucepan and sauté the mushrooms and onion, covered, for about 10 minutes on a low/medium heat. Add the tomatoes and yeast extract, breaking up the tomatoes while stirring them in and ensuring that the yeast extract is evenly dissolved into the mixture. Then add the tomato purée, herbs, nuts, breadcrumbs and wheatgerm. Mix well and season to taste. Finally, mix the soya flour and arrowroot to a smooth paste with a little cold water and add to the rest of the ingredients, blending them together thoroughly. Turn into a well-greased 2 lb (1kg) loaf tin and bake for 50–55 minutes. Leave for 5 minutes or so in the tin after removing from the oven before turning out onto a serving dish.

This is delicious with roast or baked potatoes, ginger-glazed carrots (page 135), a steamed green vegetable and savoury brown sauce (page 126).

Carrot and Hazelnut Roast

Serves 6-8

1 lb (450g) carrots, scrubbed and sliced
1 medium onion, finely chopped
1 clove garlic, crushed
4 oz (100g) mushrooms, chopped
1 tablespoon vegetable oil
1 small *or* ½ large red pepper, diced
1 teaspoon fresh, *or* ½ teaspoon dried rosemary, chopped
1 teaspoon mace
½ teaspoon paprika
1 oz (25g) vegan margarine
6 oz (175g) hazelnuts, toasted, skinned and ground
4 oz (100g) fresh, wholemeal breadcrumbs
1 tablespoon soya flour
1 tablespoon arrowroot
1 tablespoon freshly squeezed lemon juice
Black pepper and salt

Preheat the oven to 180°C (350°F, Gas 4). Place the carrots in just enough water to cover them and simmer until very soft. Meanwhile, sauté the onion, garlic and mushrooms in the oil for 5–7 minutes, using a large saucepan. Add the red pepper, rosemary, mace and paprika and continue cooking for a further 3–4 minutes. Remove from heat.

When the carrots are cooked, drain and reserve any stock, then mash them with the margarine. Add this to the sautéed vegetables together with the nuts, breadcrumbs and lemon juice, and mix well. If the mixture seems a little stiff, add a little reserved stock from the carrots to achieve a moist but fairly firm consistency. Mix the soya flour and arrowroot to a thin paste with a tablespoon of the cooled stock or water, and stir well into the rest of the ingredients until evenly blended.

Grease a 2 lb (1kg) loaf tin with margarine and press in the mixture. Cover the top with foil and bake for 50–60 minutes in the centre of the oven.

Allow the roast to cool slightly in the tin for about 10 minutes before turning out. Garnish with red pepper rings (these can be carefully overlapped at the bottom of the tin and cooked with the roast for a ready decorative finish if desired) and a few whole hazelnuts along the top of the roast.

This attractive centrepiece for a meal is delicious with roast potatoes or sesame glazed parsnips, a steamed green vegetable and a savoury brown or mushroom sauce (pages 126 and 125).

Aubergine and Brazil Nut Bake

Serves 4

2 medium aubergines
2 tablespoons oil
1 oz (25g) vegan
  margarine
6 oz (175g) mushrooms,
  cleaned and chopped
1½ teaspoons oregano
1 bunch spring onions,
  chopped
8 oz (225g) tomatoes,
  skinned and chopped
12 oz (350g) tofu
  'ricotta' cheese (see
  page 38)
Black pepper and salt
4 oz (100g) brazil nuts,
  chopped
2 oz (50g) wholemeal
  breadcrumbs
2 tablespoons fresh,
  chopped parsley
1 quantity cheese sauce
  (see page 124)
1½ oz (37g) vegan hard
  cheese (see page 35),
  grated

Slice the aubergines into ¼-inch (½cm) thick slices and place in a colander. Sprinkle generously with salt and leave to stand for 30 minutes. Rinse thoroughly under a running tap for a few minutes to remove salt and bitter tasting fluids, then pat dry. Heat a little of the oil in a large frying pan and sauté the aubergine slices in batches for 2–3 minutes on each side. Add a little more oil after each batch, but take care not to use more than the stated 2 tablespoons altogether, or the aubergines will become greasy. Place the cooked slices on kitchen paper and keep to one side.

Melt the margarine in a medium saucepan and cook the mushrooms with the oregano for 8–10 minutes over a low heat. Stir in the spring onions and tomatoes, replace lid and leave to cool, then stir in tofu ricotta cheese and season with black pepper and salt.

Preheat the oven to 180°C (350°F, Gas 4). Mix the brazil nuts with the breadcrumbs and parsley in a bowl. Grease or oil a 3½–4 pint (2–2.5 litre) casserole and spoon in half the ricotta mixture. Sprinkle half the brazil nut mixture over this and then cover with a layer of aubergine slices. Repeat the layers, ending with a ring of overlapping aubergine slices around the edge of the dish. Pour over the cheese sauce and sprinkle with the grated cheese. Bake for 30–35 minutes.

Serve with jacket potatoes and a steamed vegetable, or hot crusty bread and a side salad.

Savoury Nutmeat

Makes approximately
1½ lb (675g) nutmeat

6 oz (175g) mixed nuts
2 oz (50g) sunflower
seeds
½ oz (12g) vegan
margarine
1 tablespoon sunflower
oil
1 large onion, finely
chopped
2 oz (50g) mushrooms,
finely chopped
A good pinch each of
dried rosemary and
basil
1 rounded teaspoon
yeast extract
1 dessertspoon soy
sauce
3 tomatoes, skinned
and chopped
3 oz (75g) cooked,
mashed carrot
1 oz (25g) wholemeal
breadcrumbs
1 oz (25g) fine or
medium oatmeal
1 tablespoon soya flour
1 tablespoon arrowroot
Black pepper and salt
Sesame seeds and/or
oatmeal for coating

Spread the nuts and seeds on a baking sheet and place under a moderate grill to toast very lightly for 3–4 minutes, turning occasionally. Allow to cool, then grind quite finely (unless a grainier texture is desired). Heat the margarine and oil together in a large covered saucepan and cook the onion, mushrooms and herbs for 8–10 minutes over a low/medium heat. Stir in the yeast extract until evenly blended, then add the soy sauce, tomatoes and mashed carrot. Fold the nuts, breadcrumbs and oatmeal into the mixture, using a wooden spoon to mix the ingredients thoroughly together.

Mix the soya flour and arrowroot to a thin paste with a little water and fold well in to bind the nutmeat adequately. Season to taste and shape the mixture into sausages, burgers or cutlets. Coat the shapes with oatmeal or sesame seeds (or a mixture of these), and grill, bake or shallow-fry for a few minutes on each side, until lightly and evenly browned.

Serve with, for example, tomato, barbecue or savoury brown sauce (see pages 127, 129 and 126), together with mashed, jacket or roast potatoes and one or two steamed vegetables.

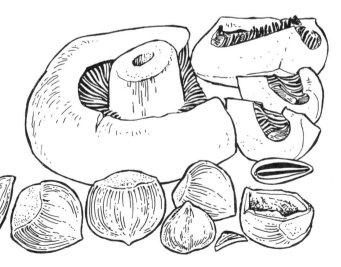

Spinach, Peanut and Tomato Layer

Serves 4

1½ lb (675g) spinach, fresh or frozen
1½ oz (37g) vegan margarine
4 oz (100g) button mushrooms, wiped and sliced
1 medium onion, chopped
1 clove garlic, crushed
1 teaspoon dried basil
½ teaspoon dried oregano
Black pepper and salt
4 oz (100g) fresh, wholemeal breadcrumbs
4 oz (100g) vegan hard cheese (see page 35), grated
5 oz (150g) roasted peanuts, rinsed, patted dry and chopped
1 × 14 oz (400g) tin tomatoes

If using fresh spinach, trim and wash thoroughly. Place in a saucepan with only 1 tablespoon extra water. Simmer, covered, on a low heat for 5–7 minutes. Then turn onto a chopping board and, when cool enough, chop finely. If using frozen spinach, thaw, drain off any excess moisture and chop finely.

Melt the margarine in a medium or large saucepan and add the mushrooms, onion, garlic and herbs. Cook over a low-medium heat, covered, for 8–10 minutes. Stir in the spinach, season to taste, and set aside.

Next, mix the breadcrumbs, peanuts and cheese in a large bowl. Liquidize the tomatoes with their juice in a blender or food processor.

Preheat the oven to 190°C (375°F, Gas 5). Grease a 3 pint (1.5 litre) casserole dish (preferably transparent, to show the layers). Spread half the spinach and mushroom mixture over the base. Pour half the liquidized tomatoes over this and then sprinkle over half the nut and breadcrumb mixture. Repeat the layers, ending with the nuts and breadcrumbs, and bake for 50–60 minutes.

Serve hot with jacket potatoes and a barbecue or rich tomato sauce (see pages 129 and 127).

Quick Vegetable and Nuttolene Fricassée

Serves 3-4

1 tablespoon sunflower *or* safflower oil
2 oz (50g) mushrooms, wiped and sliced
1 bunch spring onions, trimmed, washed and chopped
½ teaspoon dried tarragon
½ teaspoon dried basil
½ red pepper, diced
3 oz (75g) sweetcorn kernels
½ × 10 oz (275g) tin Nuttolene, diced
1 tablespoon fresh, chopped parsley *or* 1 teaspoon dried parsley
1 oz (25g) vegan margarine
1 rounded tablespoon fine-milled, wholemeal flour
1 level teaspoon mustard powder
8 fl oz (225ml) soya milk
4 fl oz (100ml) vegetable stock
Black pepper and salt
1 packet wholewheat crisps plus 1 oz (25g) grated vegan cheese (see page 35), *or* 1 oz (25g) sesame seeds

Preheat the oven to 180°C (350°F, Gas 4). Heat the oil in a large saucepan, cover and gently cook the mushrooms for 8–10 minutes. Add the spring onions and dried herbs, and continue cooking for a further 3–4 minutes. Then stir in the red pepper, sweetcorn, nuttolene and fresh parsley, replace the lid and remove from the heat till needed.

Melt the margarine in a medium saucepan and stir in the flour and mustard powder to form a roux. Add the soya milk a little at a time, followed by the vegetable stock, stirring constantly until the sauce has thickened. Season to taste.

Transfer the vegetable and nuttolene mixture into an ovenproof serving dish, pour over the sauce and top with the crisps and then the grated cheese, or with a sprinkling of sesame seeds. Place in oven for 15–20 minutes until heated through and the topping toasted. (Alternatively, the fricassée can be placed under a medium hot grill for a few minutes if the two parts of the dish are kept hot before turning into a pre-warmed serving dish.)

This is delicious with mashed potatoes and a steamed vegetable or cooked beetroot salad (see page 115).

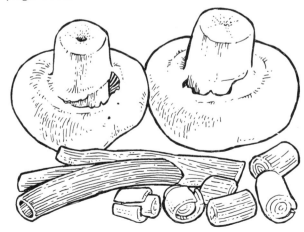

Stuffed Aubergines

Serves 4

2 medium/large aubergines
1 oz (25g) vegan margarine
4 shallots, chopped
2 oz (50g) mushrooms, chopped
1 teaspoon fresh basil
A good pinch of cayenne pepper
3 oz (75g) chopped mixed nuts
3 spring onions, chopped
2 oz (50g) fresh wholemeal breadcrumbs
6 oz (175g) vegan hard cheese (see page 35), grated
Black pepper and salt
Extra grated cheese to garnish

Wash and trim the tops off the aubergines and cut them in half lengthways. Scoop out the flesh, leaving the sides of the shells about $\frac{1}{2}$ inch (1cm) thick. Sprinkle the insides of the shells and the scooped-out flesh with salt and leave for 30 minutes, then rinse thoroughly in cold water. Blanch the shells for 4–5 minutes in a pan containing about $\frac{1}{2}$ inch (1cm) depth of simmering water. Drain and arrange in a lightly greased ovenproof dish. Chop the scooped-out aubergine flesh quite finely.

Melt the margarine in the same pan and sauté the shallots with the mushrooms, aubergine flesh, basil, and cayenne pepper, covered, for 8–10 minutes. Meanwhile, grind 2 oz (50g) of the mixed nuts. Add the spring onion to the pan and cook for another minute or two. Remove from the heat and stir in the ground and chopped nuts, breadcrumbs, and cheese. Season to taste and fill the aubergine shells with the mixture. Keep to one side while preparing the sauce.

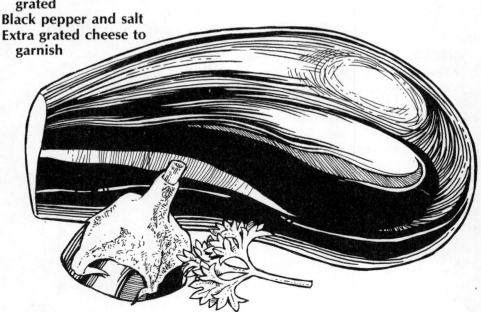

Sauce:

**4 oz (100g) button
  mushrooms, thinly
  sliced**
1 dessertspoon olive oil
**A pinch each of dried
  thyme and oregano**
**1 × 14 oz (400g) tin
  tomatoes, liquidized**
**1 tablespoon tomato
  purée**
**1 level teaspoon
  *Vecon stock
  concentrate, *or* 1
  vegetable stock cube**
1 bay leaf
**1 tablespoon fresh,
  chopped parsley**
Black pepper

Preheat the oven to 180°C (350°F, Gas 4). Cook the mushrooms, covered, in the oil with the herbs for 7–8 minutes. Add the liquidized tomatoes and tomato purée, then stir in the stock concentrate or crumbled stock-cube until dissolved. Add the bay leaf and parsley, bring gently to the boil, and simmer for 10–15 minutes. Remove the bay leaf, season with a little black pepper and pour over the filled aubergines. Scatter a little extra grated cheese over the dish and bake for 30–35 minutes.

Note: For a crispier top to the filled aubergines, sprinkle them with the extra cheese and cook without the sauce, which can then be served separately in a warmed jug or sauceboat.

* 'Vecon' is the name of a commercially-made stock concentrate, available from health-food stores and some supermarkets.

Sweet and Savoury Picnic Balls

Makes 22–24 balls

4 oz (100g) chopped, mixed nuts

Pared rind of half an orange

Pared rind of half a lemon

8 oz (225g) curd cheese (see page 37)

½ teaspoon ground fenugreek

2 teaspoons freshly squeezed lemon juice

2 oz (50g) alfalfa sprouts, chopped

2 oz (50g) grated carrot, *or* finely diced red pepper

2 oz (50g) sultanas

2 dessertspoons sunflower seeds

1 rounded tablespoon chopped, fresh chives

2 oz (50g) sesame seeds, *or* 1 oz (25g) sesame seeds mixed with 1 oz (25g) toasted desiccated coconut, to coat

The sutble contrasts of taste and texture in these easily-made additions to the picnic hamper make them a popular, refreshing snack at any time.

Grind $\frac{2}{3}$–$\frac{3}{4}$ of the nuts together with the orange and lemon rinds. Tip into a large mixing bowl and beat in the curd cheese, fenugreek and lemon juice. Fold in the rest of the nuts and the remaining ingredients (apart from those to be used for coating), then chill the mixture for 45–60 minutes. After this time, mix well again and shape small quantities into about two dozen 1-inch (2.5cm) balls.

Spread the sesame seeds or sesame-coconut mixture on a plate and lightly coat each ball, finishing with a brief rolling motion between the palms to ensure an even covering.

Store, chilled, in an airtight container until required.

Note: Other sprouts, such as mung bean sprouts, can be substituted for alfalfa if necessary.

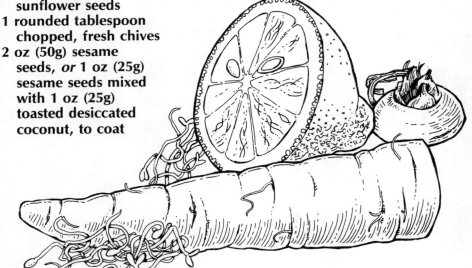

Seed and grain dishes

Aubergine and Almond Couscous

Serves 4

2 medium aubergines
2 leeks, sliced *or* 1 large
  onion, chopped
2 cloves garlic, crushed
1 teaspoon cinnamon
2 teaspoons mustard
  seeds
1 teaspoon coriander
$\frac{1}{2}$ teaspoon turmeric
1 teaspoon cumin
2 tablespoons vegetable
  oil
10 oz (275g) courgettes,
  sliced
1 large red pepper,
  diced
10 oz (275g) tomatoes,
  skinned and chopped
3 oz (75g) flaked
  almonds
2 oz (50g) raisins
3 fl oz (75ml) water
8 oz (225g) couscous
$\frac{1}{2}$ oz (12g) soft vegan
  margarine
Salt

Wash, trim and thickly dice the aubergines into chunks about $\frac{3}{4}$-1 inch (2–2.5cm) in size. Place in a colander or on a plate and sprinkle liberally with salt. Leave to stand for at least 30 minutes, then rinse well. Meanwhile, fry the leeks or onion, garlic, seeds and spices in the oil for 3–4 minutes. Stir in the rinsed aubergines and the courgettes, red pepper, tomatoes, almonds, raisins and water.

Place the couscous in a fine-meshed sieve and pour boiling water over until it is thoroughly soaked. Set the sieve over the vegetables if there is enough room in the pan without the vegetable mixture touching the bottom of the sieve. If not, set the full sieve over (not touching) simmering water in a separate covered pan. Cover the vegetables with a lid or with foil if a lid will not fit over the sieve, and cook over a low heat for 25 minutes, stirring the vegetable mixture occasionally.

When cooked, fluff up the couscous grains with a fork and mix in the margarine and a little salt. Turn onto a warmed serving dish, arranging the bulk of it around the edges, and pour the vegetable mixture onto the middle area. Serve immediately.

Nut and Seed Croustade with Mushroom and Tomato Sauce

Serves 4

4 oz (100g) chopped, mixed nuts
2 oz (50g) cashew nut pieces
1 oz (25g) sunflower seeds
2 teaspoons poppy seeds
1 tablespoon sesame seeds
1 dessertspoon wheatgerm
5 oz (150g) wholemeal breadcrumbs
2 oz (50g) vegan margarine
1 teaspoon fresh, chopped thyme, *or* $\frac{1}{2}$ **teaspoon dried thyme**
1 teaspoon fresh, chopped marjoram, *or* $\frac{1}{2}$ **teaspoon dried marjoram**
Black pepper, and salt if required

Preheat the oven to 200°C (400°F, Gas 6). Spread the nuts, seeds and wheatgerm on a baking sheet and toast lightly under a medium grill for 5–10 minutes, turning occasionally.

Place the breadcrumbs in a large bowl and rub in the margarine. Then stir in the toasted mixture and the herbs. Season with black pepper and salt to taste, and press the mixture into a lightly oiled ovenproof dish. Bake for about 20 minutes.

Sauce:
- 1 tablespoon vegetable oil
- 4 oz (100g) mushrooms, wiped and sliced
- 1 clove garlic, crushed
- 1 large or 2 small leeks, trimmed, washed and sliced fairly thinly
- 1 × 14 oz (400g) tin tomatoes, liquidized
- 2 tablespoons tomato purée
- ½ teaspoon ground bay leaves
- 1 tablespoon fresh parsley, finely chopped
- Black pepper and salt
- 1 tablespoon chopped parsley and 1 dessertspoon sesame seeds to garnish

Meanwhile, make the sauce topping. Heat the oil in a covered saucepan and sauté the mushrooms and garlic for 5–7 minutes over a low/medium heat. Add the leeks and continue cooking for a further 4–5 minutes. Pour in the liquidized tomatoes and stir in the tomato purée and ground bay leaves. Simmer uncovered for 10–15 minutes until the sauce is slightly thickened. Stir in the parsley for the last 2–3 minutes of cooking time, then season to taste and pour over the hot croustade. Garnish with a sprinkling of parsley followed by another of sesame seeds.

Serve with jacket potatoes and an accompanying vegetable such as minted courgettes and mange-touts (see page 136).

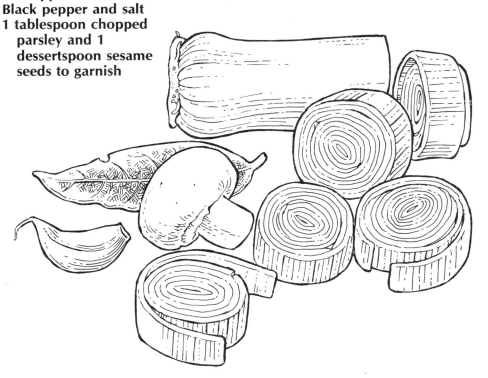

Pistachio Risotto Verde

Serves 4

6 oz (175g) long-grain
  brown rice
1 tablespoon olive oil
1 clove garlic, crushed
4–5 spring onions, *or* 1
  medium/large leek
1 pint (575ml) vegetable
  stock
1 bouquet garni (fresh
  or dried)
3 oz (75g) broccoli
  florets, cut into quite
  small pieces
3 oz (75g) cucumber,
  diced
2 oz (50g) small garden
  peas *or* french green
  beans, cut into ½-inch
  (1cm) segments
2 oz (50g) shelled
  pistachio nuts
1 tablespoon fresh
  parsley, finely
  chopped
1 oz (25g) watercress,
  finely chopped
Black pepper and salt
1½–2 oz (37–50g) vegan
  hard cheese (page
  35), grated

Rinse the rice thoroughly in a sieve and, using a large saucepan, toss it in the heated oil with the garlic for a few minutes until lightly toasted. Slice the spring onions or leek into segments or rings, add to the pan and cook for a further 1–2 minutes. Pour in the stock and add the bouquet garni. Bring to the boil, then reduce the heat and simmer, covered, for 25 minutes. Stir in the remaining ingredients, replace the lid and cook for a further 10–15 minutes, until all the liquid has been absorbed and the vegetables are tender but not stewed. Season to taste and transfer to a warmed serving dish. Sprinkle over the grated cheese and serve.

Golden Aduki and Millet Crumble

Serves 4

5 oz (150g) aduki beans
2 oz (50g) millet grains
2–3 leeks, washed, trimmed and sliced
4 oz (100g) mushrooms, wiped and sliced
1 tablespoon oil
2 medium carrots, peeled and chopped into sticks
2 medium or 1 large parsnip, peeled and chopped into sticks
$\frac{1}{2}$ teaspoon dried rosemary
$\frac{1}{2}$ teaspoon dried thyme
3 tablespoons soy sauce
2 tablespoons tomato purée
1 teaspoon miso (or yeast extract)
1 tablespoon chopped, fresh parsley
Black pepper and salt

Crumble topping:
3 oz (75g) wholemeal flour
2 oz (50g) porridge oats
1 oz (25g) millet flakes
$2\frac{1}{2}$ oz (62g) vegan margarine
1 tablespoon sunflower or sesame seeds (optional)

Soak aduki beans overnight or hot soak (page 183). Then drain, rinse well and bring to boil in $1\frac{1}{2}$ pints (850ml) fresh water. Simmer for 40–50 minutes until tender. Rinse the millet grains thoroughly in a sieve and set aside. Meanwhile, in a large, covered saucepan, sauté the leeks and mushrooms in the oil for 8–10 minutes over a low-medium heat. Add the aduki beans with their stock, the rinsed millet grains, carrots, parsnips, herbs, soy sauce, tomato purée and miso or yeast extract. Simmer uncovered for about 15 minutes until millet grains have become swollen and fluffy and the mixture has thickened slightly. Stir in the parsley, cover and remove from heat. Preheat the oven to 190°C (375°F, Gas 5).

To make the crumble, sift the flour into a bowl and stir in the oats and millet flakes. Rub in the margarine until the mixture resembles coarse breadcrumbs. Toss in the seeds if using. Transfer the aduki-millet mixture into a 3-pint (2 litre) ovenproof dish. Sprinkle the crumble topping over to cover evenly and bake for 20–25 minutes.

Serve immediately, on its own or with mashed potatoes or steamed vegetables.

Nutty Paella

Serves 4

1 large onion, sliced
  lengthwise into strips
2 cloves garlic, crushed
2 oz (50g) whole
  cashew nuts
2 oz (50g) split almonds
2 tablespoons vegetable
  oil
6 oz (175g) long-grain
  brown rice
1½ teaspoons dried
  basil, *or* 3 teaspoons
  fresh, chopped basil
½ teaspoon dried
  rosemary, *or* 1
  teaspoon chopped
  fresh rosemary
1 × 14 oz (400g) tin
  tomatoes, run
  through a sieve or
  liquidized
½ pint (275ml) tomato
  juice
½ pint (275ml) hot
  water
2 medium carrots
  peeled and cut into
  julienne strips
2 small/medium
  courgettes, cut
  lengthwise into strips
1 red pepper, sliced
  vertically into strips
1 heaped tablespoon
  fresh parsley
A squeeze of lemon
  juice
Black pepper and salt

Sauté the onion, garlic and nuts in the oil for 4–5 minutes until the onion is softened and the nuts are slightly toasted. Add the washed and drained rice and the herbs and cook for a further 2–3 minutes, stirring occasionally. Pour in the sieved tomatoes, tomato juice and water, bring to the boil and simmer, covered, for 15 minutes. Add the vegetables and cook for another 15–20 minutes, adding the parsley for the last 5 minutes of cooking time. Stir in the lemon juice, season to taste and transfer to a warmed serving dish. Garnish with a sprinkling of parsley, olives and/or wedges of lemon, if desired.

Stuffed Courgettes with Almond and Rosemary Sauce

Serves 4

4 oz (100g) millet grains
4 medium/large
  courgettes
1 oz (25g) vegan
  margarine
1 medium onion, finely
  chopped
2 cloves garlic, crushed
4 oz (100g) mushrooms,
  chopped
$\frac{1}{2}$ teaspoon cut, dried
  bay leaves
$\frac{1}{2}$ teaspoon dried thyme
1 level teaspoon ground
  coriander
1 red pepper, diced
Black pepper and salt
1 quantity almond and
  rosemary sauce (see
  page 127)

Rinse the millet grains thoroughly in a sieve and cook in twice their volume (8–9 fl oz or 225–250ml) of simmering water for 15 minutes. Then turn out into a sieve to drain off any excess water and allow the grains to cool slightly.

Top and tail the courgettes and blanch them in boiling water for about 3 minutes. Drain, allow to cool a little and cut them in half along their lengths. Scoop out the fleshy centres, chop the removed flesh and keep to one side.

Preheat the oven to 180°C (350°F, Gas 4). Melt the margarine in a covered pan and sauté the onion, garlic, mushrooms and herbs for 4–5 minutes. Add the chopped courgette flesh, coriander and red pepper and cook for another 1–2 minutes. Remove from heat and stir in the millet grains. Season to taste and fill the courgettes with this mixture. Arrange in a lightly oiled ovenproof dish, cover with foil and bake for 25–30 minutes.

Serve hot with almond and rosemary sauce.

Mixed Grain Ring

Serves 6–8

1 tablespoon oil
2 oz (50g) long-grain
   brown rice
1 pint (575ml) boiling
   water
2 oz (50g) buckwheat
   groats
2 oz (50g) millet grains
1 large onion, chopped
1 clove garlic
1 teaspoon mustard
   seed
1 teaspoon mace
1 teaspoon paprika
6–7 oz (175–200g)
   sweet potato
   (preferably the type
   with pink-orange
   flesh), diced
3 sticks celery, chopped
2 oz (50g) hazelnuts,
   toasted, skinned and
   chopped or crushed
2 oz (50g) sultanas
2 tablespoons cold
   water
1 tablespoon sherry
   (optional)
Black pepper and salt
Sliced tomatoes and
   watercress or parsley
   to garnish (optional)

Rinse the rice thoroughly in a sieve and fry in a few drops of the oil for 2–3 minutes, using a medium/large saucepan. Pour in the boiling water and simmer, covered, for 10 minutes. After this time, add the rinsed buckwheat and millet and cook for a further 15 minutes. Then drain any excess water from the grains and keep aside.

Preheat the oven to 180°C (350°F, Gas 4). While the grains are cooking, sauté the onion, garlic, mustard seed and spices in the rest of the oil for 4–5 minutes. Add the sweet potato and celery and cook for another 5–7 minutes over a low heat. Stir in the hazelnuts and sultanas. Mix the grains and vegetables together, add the cold water and sherry if using, and season to taste. Pile this mixture into a greased 9-inch (22cm) ring tin, cover with foil and bake for 45 minutes.

Turn out, pile the garnish ingredients in the centre and serve hot with curry sauce (see page 128).

Tomato-baked Nori Roulade

Serves 6

4 oz (100g) long-grain brown rice
2 oz (50g) walnuts
2 oz (50g) brazil nuts *or* almonds
1 lb (450g) tofu ricotta cheese (see page 38)
1 bunch (7–8) spring onions, chopped
1 small red pepper, finely diced
2 tablespoons soy sauce
½ teaspoon ground bay leaves
2 tomatoes, chopped
Black pepper and salt
6 sheets shushi nori
1 quantity rich tomato sauce (see page 127)
Extra chopped nuts to garnish (optional)

Cook the rice, covered, in twice its volume of boiling water for 25–30 minutes until tender and the water absorbed.

Meanwhile, preheat the oven to 180°C (350°F, Gas 4). Grind or very finely chop the nuts and mix them with the cooked rice, tofu ricotta, spring onions, red pepper, soy sauce, ground bay leaves and tomatoes. Season to taste with black pepper and salt and use this mixture to spread over one side of each sheet of shushi nori. Roll up the nori like a swiss roll. Arrange the 6 filled sheets in a lightly oiled shallow square or rectangular ovenproof dish (at least 9 inches or 22cm wide to accommodate the length of the rolled nori). Pour over the tomato sauce, cover with foil and bake for 30–35 minutes.

Garnish with a sprinkling of extra chopped nuts if desired and serve hot with jacket potatoes; tofu pasta-noodles (see page 94); or extra, freshly cooked brown rice.

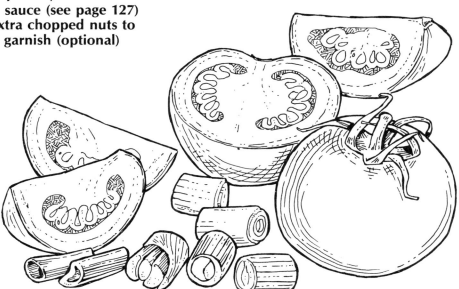

Pasta, pancakes and pastry dishes

Tofu Pasta-noodles

***Makes approximately
1 lb (450g) noodles***

**8 oz (225g) firm tofu
2 tablespoons sunflower
oil
8 oz (225g) fine-milled,
wholewheat flour
1 tablespoon soya flour
$\frac{1}{2}$ teaspoon salt**

Blend the tofu with the oil until smooth and creamy in a liquidizer or food processor, or with an electric hand-whisk.

Sift the flours and salt together and combine with the tofu mixture, kneading well together until a soft dough forms.

Cover and leave the dough to rest for 15–20 minutes, then roll out thinly on a floured surface and cut into desired pasta or noodle shapes (this can be done with a pasta-cutting machine if available, or with shaped cutting devices such as a ravioli press, or simply by hand with a knife).

Leave the rolled and cut pasta noodles to dry for 20 minutes or so before cooking. If not required immediately, cover with cling-film and keep in a refrigerator until needed. You can also freeze them.

To prepare, cook for 5–7 minutes in a pan of boiling water, to which 1 teaspoon of oil has been added to prevent any sticking.

This mixture makes a super base for shaping into cannelloni, ravioli, lasagne and so forth, as well as providing a good alternative to egg-noodles as an accompaniment to Oriental or Chinese dishes and stir-fries.

This recipe can be varied by adding 3–4 oz (75–100g) of finely chopped, cooked spinach to the mixture and increasing the amount of flour by about 1 oz (25g).

Lentil and Chestnut Tagliatelle

Serves 4

4 oz (100g) dried
  chestnuts
1 bay leaf
4 oz (100g) continental
  lentils
1 oz (25g) vegan
  margarine
4 oz (100g) mushrooms,
  sliced or chopped
1 medium onion, sliced
  into rings
1 clove garlic, crushed
1 teaspoon oregano
3 tablespoons soy sauce
4 tablespoons red wine
6 oz (175g) tomatoes,
  skinned and chopped
2 tablespoons tomato
  purée
1 red pepper, diced
  (optional)
2 tablespoons fresh
  parsley, finely
  chopped
12 oz (350g)
  wholewheat
  tagliatelle
Black pepper and salt

Rinse the chestnuts and simmer in $1\frac{1}{4}$ pints (725ml) water with the bay leaf for 1 hour until tender. During this time, remove any grit or stones from the lentils, rinse them thoroughly in a sieve and add to the chestnuts for the last 20 minutes of cooking time.

Melt the margarine in a separate pan and cook the mushrooms, covered for 7–10 minutes. Add the onion, garlic and oregano, and continue to cook for a further 4–5 minutes. Mash or break up the cooked chestnuts a little and stir these, together with the lentils, bay leaf and stock, the soy sauce and red wine, into the mushroom mixture. Bring to the boil and simmer for 15 minutes, then add the tomatoes, tomato purée, red pepper if using, and half the parsley. Simmer for a further 10–15 minutes until the lentils are fully tender. During the last 10 minutes of this time, cook the tagliatelle in plenty of boiling water, to which a few drops of oil have been added, for 8–10 minutes. Drain and transfer to a warmed serving dish. Season the lentil and chestnut sauce with a little black pepper and salt and pour over the tagliatelle. Sprinkle over the remaining parsley, and decorate, if desired, with a few rings or diced pieces of red pepper before serving.

Superb with a crisp salad and hot French or garlic bread.

Spinach and Almond Lasagne

Serves 4–6

1½ lb (675g) spinach,
  fresh or frozen
1 oz (25g) vegan
  margarine
1 large onion, chopped
2 cloves garlic, crushed
1½ teaspoons dried
  marjoram
1 teaspoon dried thyme
¼ pint (150ml) hot
  water
A pinch of nutmeg
4 oz (100g) ground
  almonds
4 oz (100g) nibbed or
  chopped almonds
Black pepper and salt
9 strips wholewheat
  lasagne
1 × 14 oz (400g) tin
  tomatoes, chopped
Toasted flaked *or*
  nibbed almonds to
  garnish

Trim, wash and roughly chop the spinach if fresh, and blanch it for 8–10 minutes in just enough water to cover the bottom of the pan. Drain and allow to cool slightly, then chop quite finely. If using frozen spinach, thaw and chop finely.

Melt the margarine in a medium saucepan and cook the onion, garlic and herbs in it for 7–8 minutes. Stir in the chopped spinach, water, nutmeg and almonds. Mix well, season with black pepper and salt, cover and set aside.

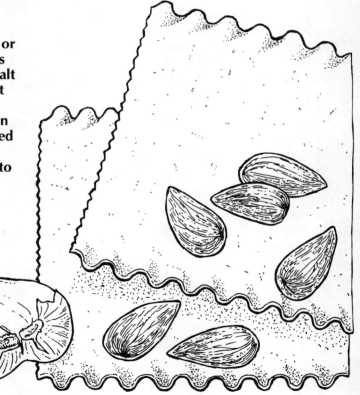

Mushroom sauce:
8 oz (225g) button
  mushrooms, wiped
  and thinly sliced
1½ oz (37g) vegan
  margarine
1 oz (25g) fine-milled
  wholemeal flour
1 dessertspoon soya
  flour
½ pint (275ml) soya
  milk
¼ pint (150ml) strong
  vegetable stock, *or* ¼
  pint (150ml) hot
  water plus 1 rounded
  teaspoon Vecon* or a
  vegetable stock cube
Black pepper and salt

Next, make the sauce. Sauté the mushrooms in the heated margarine, covered, for 10–12 minutes, until tender and juicy. Meanwhile, dissolve the Vecon or stock cube, if using, in the hot water. When the mushrooms are cooked, reduce the heat to low and stir in the flours to make a roux. Gradually add the soya milk, stirring constantly to prevent lumps from forming. When all the milk has been added pour in the stock and increase the heat, still stirring until sauce thickens. Season to taste and cover till needed.

Preheat the oven to 180°C (350°F, Gas 4). Cook the lasagne strips in plenty of boiling water, to which a little oil has been added, for 8–10 minutes until just tender. Drain into a colander and rinse under running cold water to stop further cooking and prevent sticking. Lay 3 strips of lasagne along the bottom of a greased rectangular 3–4 pint (1¾–2½l) ovenproof dish (preferably about 7 × 11 inches or 18 × 28cm). Cover with half the spinach and almond mixture, then with half the chopped tin of tomatoes, and finally with a third of the mushroom sauce. Repat the layers once more, and top with the final 3 strips of lasagne covered with the remaining third of the mushroom sauce. Sprinkle with the lightly toasted almond flakes or nibs, cover with foil or a lid if available, and bake for 45–50 minutes. Serve hot with a crisp, colourful salad and warm crusty french bread.

* Vecon is the name of a commercially-made stock concentrate, available from health-food stores and some supermarkets.

Pepperoni Pizza

***Makes 2 generously
    topped 10–12 inch
    (25–30cm) pizzas***

Base:
**8 oz (225g) wholemeal
    flour**
1 tablespoon soya flour
Pinch salt
**1 oz (25g) vegan
    margarine**
½ teaspoon maple syrup
½ oz (12g) fresh yeast
**¼ pint (150ml)
    lukewarm water**

To make the base, sift the flours and salt together in a bowl. Rub in the margarine. Stir the maple syrup and yeast into the water and mix well. Leave in a warm place for 8–10 minutes, until frothy, then pour into the flour mixture and fold in with a wooden spoon until a dough forms. Knead this in the bowl for about 5 minutes, then cover with lightly oiled cling-film or a warm, damp tea-towel and put in a warm place for an hour or so until doubled in size.

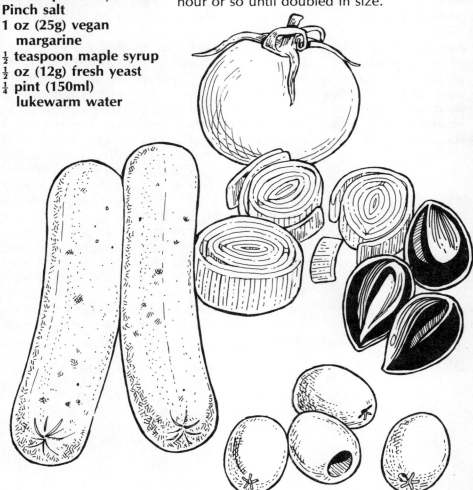

Topping:

- **7–8 vegan sausages, either tinned or made from approx. 8 oz (225g) nutmeat mixture (see page 79)**
- **2 tablespoons wholemeal flour**
- **2 tablespoons paprika**
- **$\frac{1}{4}$–$\frac{1}{2}$ teaspoon chilli powder**
- **2 tablespoons olive oil**
- **1 leek, finely sliced**
- **1 clove garlic, crushed**
- **1 teaspoon dried marjoram**
- **1 teaspoon dried basil**
- **1 green pepper, diced**
- **12 oz (350g) fresh tomatoes, chopped**
- **4 tablespoons tomato juice**
- **2 tablespoons tomato purée**
- **Black pepper and salt**
- **4 oz (100g) vegan hard cheese (see page 35), grated**
- **Olives, slices of tomato, diced red pepper to garnish (optional)**

Meanwhile, prepare the topping. Cut the sausages into segments approximately $\frac{1}{2}$ inch (1cm) long. Mix the flour, paprika and chilli powder on a plate and coat the sausage pieces in the mixture. Sauté in 1 tablespoon of the oil for a few minutes, turning occasionally until browned and crisp on the outside. Remove from the pan and keep aside.

Heat the other tablespoon of oil in the same pan and sauté the leek with the garlic and herbs until soft. Add the green pepper and cook for a further 2–3 minutes. Stir in the tomatoes, tomato juice and tomato purée and simmer the mixture for 10–12 minutes over a low-medium heat. Season with salt and black pepper and keep to one side. Knead the risen dough once more for 2–3 minutes until smooth and elastic. Roll it out on a floured surface to form 2 thin rounds about 10–12 inches (25–30cm) across. Place these on baking sheets lightly sprinkled with flour.

Preheat the oven to 200°C (400°F, Gas 6). Gently stir the sausage pieces into the tomato mixture and spoon half of this topping onto each of the pizza bases. Sprinkle the grated cheese over this and decorate with any or all of the suggested garnishes. Return to a warm place to rise for 10–15 minutes, then bake for 20–25 minutes, until the edges of the pizza bases are browned and puffy and the cheese is melted and golden.

Quick Unyeasted Pizza

Makes 2 × 8-inch (20cm) pizzas

Topping:
1 medium onion, chopped
1 clove garlic, crushed
4 oz (100g) mushrooms, wiped and sliced
1 tablespoon olive oil
1 courgette *or* stick of celery, thinly sliced
1 teaspoon dried oregano
2 oz (50g) sweetcorn kernels (optional)
1 × 14 oz (400g) tin tomatoes, roughly chopped
1 tablespoon tomato purée
1 tablespoon fresh parsley, finely chopped
Black pepper and salt
3 oz (75g) vegan hard cheese (see page 35), grated
Capers, black and/or green olives, slices of tomato, rings of red pepper to garnish (optional)

First, make the topping. Sauté the onion, garlic and mushrooms in the oil for 4–5 minutes over a low-medium heat. Add the courgette or celery and oregano, and continue to cook for another minute or two. Stir in the sweetcorn kernels if using, the tomatoes and tomato purée. Bring to the boil, cover and simmer for 10–15 minutes. Remove from the heat, add the parsley, season to taste, replace lid and leave to cool slightly while preparing the base.

Preheat the oven to 190°C (375°F, Gas 5).

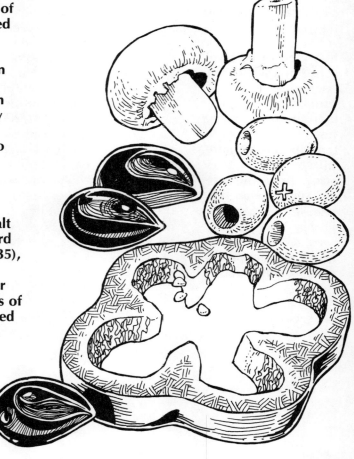

Base:
**8 oz (225g) fine-milled
wholemeal flour**
**1 teaspoon cream of
tartar**
**1 teaspoon bicarbonate
of soda**
A pinch of salt
**1½ oz (37g) vegan
margarine**
**1 tablespoon sunflower
oil**
**4–6 tablespoons cold
water**

To make the base, sift the flour, cream of tartar, bicarbonate of soda and salt together in a large bowl. Rub in the margarine until a breadcrumblike texture is obtained, then stir in the oil and enough of the water to produce a soft dough. Knead this lightly and roll out on a floured surface to form 2 rounds approximately 8 inches (20cm) in diameter. Place these on a lightly floured baking sheet or sheets, and spread each with half of the topping mixture. Sprinkle the grated cheese over the pizzas, arrange any garnishes decoratively on top and bake for 20–25 minutes.

Wheat and Barley Pancakes

Makes 8 pancakes

**2 oz (50g) wholemeal
self-raising flour**
2 oz (50g) barley flour
1 tablespoon soya flour
A pinch of salt
**6 fl oz (175ml) soya
milk**
6 fl oz (175ml) water
2 teaspoons oil
Extra oil for frying

Sift and mix the flours and salt together in a bowl. Put the soya milk, water and oil in a liquidizer and gradually add the dry ingredients, a heaped tablespoon a a time, blending well after each addition. Leave the mixture to stand for at least 30 minutes, and preferably for 1 hour or more.

When ready to cook, brush a heated frying pan with a little oil and pour in enough batter to coat the base of the pan. Cook each pancake for 3–4 minutes on each side over a moderate heat, until the two sides are lightly browned. Stack on a warmed plate, cover with foil, and leave in a low oven until ready to fill and serve.

Tofu Pancakes

Makes 8–10 pancakes

4 oz (100g) fine-milled, wholemeal flour
1 oz (25g) soya flour
2 level teaspoons baking powder
A pinch of salt
4 oz (100g) silken tofu
1 tablespoon vegetable oil
½ pint (275ml) soya milk
A little extra oil for frying

Sift the flours with the baking powder and salt into a bowl. Blend the tofu with the oil and milk in a liquidizer until smooth. Add the dry ingredients and blend again.

Brush a heated frying pan with a little oil and add about 4 tablespoons of the mixture at a time. Tilt the pan to spread the batter evenly and cook over a moderate-high heat for 3–4 minutes on each side, or until brown speckles or patches appear.

Transfer to a warmed plate, cover with foil and keep warm under a low-medium grill or in a warm oven.

Asparagus and Almond Cream Filling

Fills 6 pancakes

1 lb (450g) fresh asparagus, *or* 2 × 10½ oz (300g) cans asparagus
½ oz (12g) vegan margarine
1 small leek
1 teaspoon dried chervil, *or* 2 teaspoons fresh chervil, chopped
2 oz (50g) ground almonds

If using fresh asparagus, rinse well and remove any hard sections of stem at the base of the spears. Cut into segments of ½–¾ inch (1–2cm). If using canned asparagus, drain and cut as above.

Melt the margarine in a pan and gently cook the leek, fresh asparagus if using, and chervil, covered, for 12–15 minutes. Stir in the canned asparagus after this time. Add the ground almonds and mix well until evenly blended. Gradually stir in ½ pint (275ml) of the soya milk, then add the herbs and nutmeg, increase the heat slightly and stir until the sauce begins to thicken. Reduce the heat to low, add more soya milk if necessary (this is more likely to be needed if using fresh asparagus), cover and leave to simmer for 10–12 minutes, stirring occasionally to prevent any sticking and to check moisture level.

Season to taste with black pepper and a little

10–15 fl oz (275–425ml) soya milk
2 tablespoons mustard and cress, *or* watercress *or* parsley, finely chopped
A good pinch of nutmeg
Black pepper and salt
Toasted, flaked almonds to garnish

salt, and fill 6 pancakes with the mixture. Roll these up and arrange in a warmed serving dish. Sprinkle over a few toasted flaked almonds and serve straight away.

Note: If not serving immediately, brush the rolled pancakes with a little soya milk or juice reserved from the canned asparagus before sprinkling on the almonds. Cover with foil and keep warm in a low oven until needed.

Fennel and Mushroom Filling with Water Chestnuts

Fills 6 pancakes

1 medium bulb fennel, finely sliced (reserve any feathery tops for garnish)
½ teaspoon fennel seeds
½ teaspoon ground aniseed
1 dessertspoon oil
1 oz (25g) vegan margarine
6 oz (175g) button mushrooms, wiped and sliced
1 teaspoon dried tarragon, *or* 2 teaspoons fresh, chopped tarragon
½ teaspoon mustard powder
1 heaped tablespoon wholewheat flour
½ pint (275ml) soya milk
5–6 water chestnuts, chopped
Black pepper and salt

Sauté the fennel, seeds and aniseed in the oil for 2–3 minutes, then add 2 tablespoons water, cover, and cook on a low heat for 10–12 minutes.

Meanwhile, melt the margarine in another covered pan and sauté the mushrooms with the tarragon for 7–8 minutes. Stir in the mustard powder and flour to form a roux, then gradually add the milk and continue stirring until the sauce thickens. Add the fennel mixture and the water chestnuts and cook for a further minute or two, still stirring.

Season to taste, and use the mixture to fill 6 pancakes. Serve garnished with any reserved feathery fennel tops.

Florentine Filling

Fills 6–8 pancakes

1 lb (450g) spinach,
 trimmed and rinsed
 thoroughly
1 oz (25g) vegan
 margarine
4 shallots, *or* 1 medium
 onion, chopped
4 oz (100g) mushrooms,
 chopped
1 clove garlic, crushed
1 teaspoon dried
 marjoram, *or* 2
 teaspoons fresh
 chopped marjoram
2 oz (50g) pine-kernels
1 quantity cheese sauce
 (see page 124)
Black pepper and salt
Soya milk for brushing
Extra grated cheese and
 pine-kernels to serve

Place the freshly washed spinach in a medium-large saucepan, add a tablespoon of water and cook gently for about 7 minutes. Turn onto a chopping board and allow to cool slightly, then chop finely.

Melt margarine in the same pan and sauté the shallots or onion, mushrooms, garlic and marjoram, covered, for 5–7 minutes. Add the spinach and pine-kernels, replace lid and cook for a further 2–3 minutes, tossing ingredients together occasionally. Switch off the heat and stir in the cheese sauce. Season to taste, then use about a heaped tablespoon of the mixture to fill each pancake.

Roll the filled pancakes up and arrange with the 'join' underneath, in a lightly greased, shallow ovenproof dish. Brush the pancakes with a little soya milk and scatter the extra grated cheese over the top. Sprinkle a few pine-kernels over this and reheat in the upper part of a moderate 180°C (350°F, Gas 4) oven for 8–10 minutes.

Serve at once.

Watercress and Ricotta Filling

Fills 6–8 pancakes

Filling:
12 oz (350g) tofu
  'ricotta' cheese (see
  page 38)
3 oz (75g) finely
  chopped watercress
5 oz (150g) chopped
  tomatoes
1 teaspoon celery seeds
¼ teaspoon paprika
3 tablespoons tomato
  juice
Black pepper and salt

To serve:
1 quantity tomato sauce
  (see page 127)
Extra watercress to
  garnish

Place all filling ingredients in a medium saucepan and heat gently. Cook over a low-moderate heat for 8–10 minutes, stirring occasionally.

Fill and roll up the pancakes, place in a warmed serving dish, pour over the tomato sauce and garnish with a few sprigs of watercress. Serve immediately.

Courgette, Mushroom and Cheese Quiche

Makes 1 × 8-inch (20cm) quiche

Wholemeal pastry case:
6 oz (175g) wholemeal
  self-raising flour
A small pinch of salt
2½ oz (62g) vegan
  margarine
2 tablespoons oil
4–6 tablespoons cold
  water

Sift the flour and salt together and rub in the margarine until a breadcrumb-like texture is obtained.

Add the oil and enough of the water to produce a soft (but not sticky) dough. Knead this lightly in the bowl, then cover and leave in the refrigerator or a cool place for about 20 minutes.

Filling:

6 oz (175g) mushrooms thinly sliced or chopped
1 medium onion, chopped
½ oz (12g) vegan margarine
10 oz (275g) courgettes, diced
12 oz (350g) firm tofu
1 tablespoon soy sauce
1 tablespoon oil
2 teaspoons freshly squeezed lemon juice
4 oz (100g) grated hard cheese (see page 35)
Black pepper and salt

Meanwhile, make the filling. Gently cook the mushrooms and onion, covered, in the heated margarine for 10–12 minutes. Add the courgettes and continue to cook for a further 5–7 minutes, then remove from heat and allow to cool slightly. Blend the tofu with the soy sauce, oil and lemon juice until smooth and creamy. Fold in the vegetables and 3 oz (75g) of the grated cheese. Mix ingredients well together and season to taste.

Grease an 8-inch (20cm) flan or sponge tin. Preheat the oven to 200°C (400°F, Gas 6).

When the pastry has rested for 20 minutes or so, roll it out on a lightly floured surface to fit the prepared tin. Press it evenly onto the base and sides of the tin, then prick the base in a few places with a fork to prevent 'bubbling'. Bake the pastry-case for 6–8 minutes in the upper part of the oven, then remove and turn the oven down to 180°C (350°F, Gas 4).

Allow the pastry-case to cool for 5–10 minutes, until the oven has lowered its temperature, then pile in the prepared filling and smooth over the surface. Sprinkle on the remaining grated cheese and bake in the centre of the oven for 45–50 minutes.

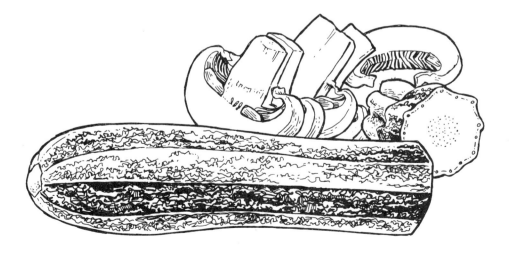

SALADS

Spiced Pasta Salad

Serves 4–6

**5 oz (150g) cucumber,
  peeled and diced
Salt
6 oz (175g) wholewheat
  pasta shells or rings
1 green pepper, diced
2 oz (50g) currants
3–4 tablespoons fresh,
  chopped chives**

Dressing:
**6 tablespoons olive oil
1½ tablespoons red
  wine vinegar
1 clove garlic, crushed
½ teaspoon ground
  cumin
½ teaspoon garam
  masala
1 level teaspoon ground
  coriander**

Sprinkle the diced cucumber with salt and leave to stand for 20 minutes, then rinse well and pat dry with kitchen paper.

Cook the pasta in plenty of boiling water, to which a few drops of oil have been added, for 8–10 minutes until just tender. Drain and rinse under cold running water to cool and halt the cooking process. Transfer to a large bowl and add the prepared cucumber, green pepper, currants and chives. Place the dressing ingredients in a liquidizer goblet and blend until frothy. Pour over the salad and toss well, taking care not to break the cooked pasta.

Italian Tofu and Tomato Salad

Serves 4

12 oz (350g) firm salad
  tomatoes, sliced into
  circles
5 oz (150g) fine green
  beans, cut into 1-inch
  (2.5cm) segments
6–7 oz (175–200g)
  cooked and drained
  red kidney beans
4 oz (100g) firm tofu,
  cut into $\frac{1}{2}$-inch (1cm)
  cubes
2–3 oz (50–75g) green
  stuffed olives, sliced
  into rings

Dressing:
4 tablespoons olive oil
1 tablespoon wine or
  tarragon vinegar
1 clove garlic, chopped
  (optional)
1 teaspoon fresh
  oregano, finely
  chopped, *or* $\frac{1}{2}$
  teaspoon dried
  oregano
Freshly ground black
  pepper

Place the salad ingredients in a large bowl.

Blend all the dressing ingredients together in a
liquidizer and pour over the salad. Toss gently
until well mixed and coated.

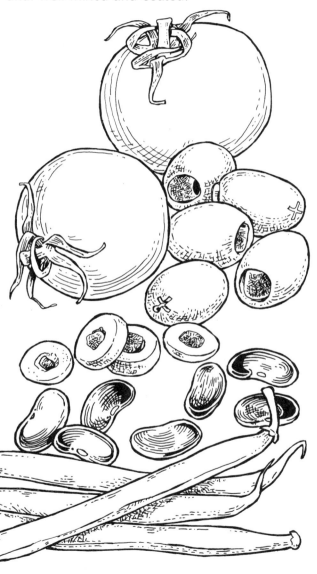

Courgette and White Bean Salad

Serves 4–6

**6 oz (175g) cannellini
  or butter beans,
  soaked overnight**
**6–7 oz (175–200g)
  courgettes, thinly
  sliced**
**2 tablespoons fresh
  parsley, finely
  chopped**
**¼ pint (150ml) soya
  yoghurt (see page 30)**
**2 teaspoons fresh,
  chopped mint**
**1 small clove garlic,
  crushed**
Black pepper and salt

Drain the soaked beans and bring to the boil in a pan of fresh water, covered to about double their height. Simmer for 40–50 minutes until just tender. Drain, rinse under cold water and place in a large mixing bowl to cool completely. Meanwhile, prepare the dressing.

Place the yoghurt in a measuring jug and fold in the mint and crushed garlic (do not use a liquidizer, as it can make the consistency too fluid). Season to taste with black pepper and salt. Add the courgettes and parsley to the cooked beans and pour over the dressing. Toss the ingredients well together until evenly coated.

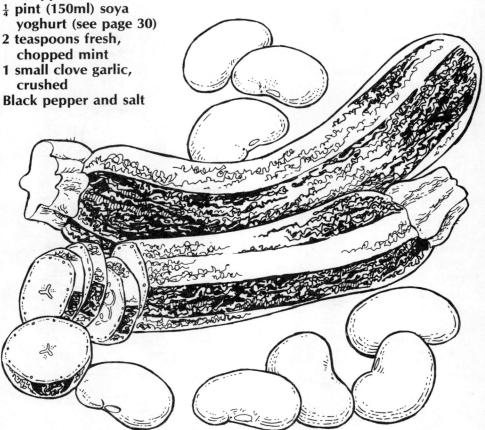

Red Cabbage, Prune and Pumpkin Slaw

Serves 6

4 oz (100g) prunes
4 fl oz (100ml) apple juice
8 oz (225g) red cabbage, finely shredded
6 oz (175g) pumpkin, *or* swede, *or* golden turnip, grated or shredded
1½ oz (37g) pumpkin seeds
6 oz (175g) seedless green grapes, halved

Dressing:

2 fl oz (50ml) sunflower oil
1 tablespoon red wine vinegar
Remaining juice from soaked prunes (about 2–3 fl oz, or 50–75ml)

Soak the prunes in the apple juice (preferably in a small bowl or a jug, so that the prunes are just covered in liquid) for 2–2½ hours.

Meanwhile, prepare the vegetables and mix them in a large bowl with the pumpkin seeds and halved grapes.

When the prunes have soaked, drain them, reserving the juice, and roughly slice or chop the flesh off the stones. Discard the stones and add the flesh to the bowl.

Put the soaking juice in a liquidizer with the rest of the dressing ingredients and blend thoroughly. Pour this onto the fruit, vegetable and seed mixture and toss well.

Raw Beetroot and Carrot Salad

Serves 4–6

8 oz (225g) raw
   beetroots, peeled and
   grated
8 oz (225g) carrots,
   peeled and grated
2 large dessert apples,
   diced
1 tablespoon freshly
   squeezed lemon juice
2 oz (50g) sultanas

Dressing:
6 tablespoons sunflower
   oil
1 tablespoon red wine
   vinegar
3 tablespoons fresh
   orange juice (from a
   carton will do)
2 level teaspoons
   ground coriander
Black pepper and salt

Put the beetroot and carrot in a large bowl. Toss the diced apple in the lemon juice and add to the bowl together with the sultanas.

Place all the dressing ingredients in a liquidizer and blend until smooth and frothy. Pour onto the salad and toss all the ingredients well together until evenly coated.

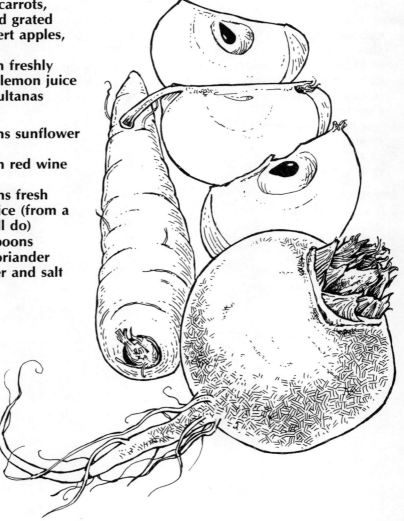

Tropical Cauliflower and Parsnip Salad

Serves 4–6

1 small or ½ large cauliflower, divided into small florets
6–8 oz (175–225g) (about 2 medium) parsnips, grated
3 oz (75g) dates, sliced fairly thinly
2 bananas, sliced
2 oz (50g) flaked almonds, toasted
1 tablespoon poppy seeds

Dressing:
6 tablespoons apple juice
2 tablespoons freshly squeezed lemon juice
2 tablespoons sunflower oil

Place all salad ingredients in a large bowl. Blend the dressing ingredients in a liquidizer and pour over the fruit and vegetables. Toss gently.

This salad is an unusual and tasty combination of flavours and textures.

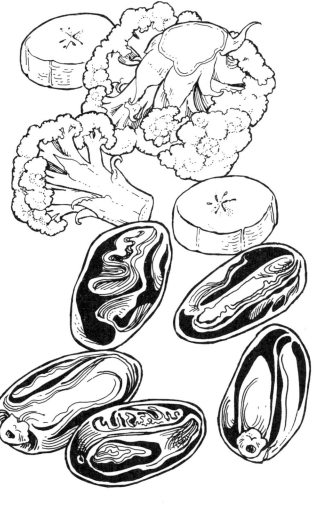

Hazelnut Rice Salad

Serves 6-8

8 oz (225g) long-grain brown rice
3 oz (75g) hazelnuts, toasted, skinned and crushed or chopped
1 medium red pepper, diced
4 oz (100g) sweetcorn kernels
3 oz (75g) button mushrooms, wiped and sliced
5-6 radishes, sliced into rings
Black pepper and salt

Dressing:
3 tablespoons sunflower oil
5 tablespoons pineapple juice
1 teaspoon root ginger, finely grated
1 tablespoon cider vinegar
$\frac{1}{4}$ teaspoon paprika

Cook the rice in plenty of boiling water for about 25 minutes until just tender.

Meanwhile, place all the dressing ingredients in a liquidizer and blend for about 15 seconds. When the rice is cooked, turn out into a sieve and rinse well with boiling water from a kettle. Shake off excess water, transfer to a bowl and immediately pour over the prepared dressing. Toss well and allow to cool slightly, then add the remaining ingredients. Toss again, season to taste and serve.

Cooked Beetroot and Mooli Salad

Serves 4-6

12 oz (350g) beetroot, cooked for 25-30 minutes
8 oz (225g) mooli, cut into julienne strips
1-2 tablespoons fresh chives, chopped
7-8 tablespons tofu soured cream (see page 34)
1 clove garlic
Black pepper and salt

Peel the cooked beetroot and cut into strips to match the mooli. Toss the two vegetables together in a bowl with the chives. Crush the garlic into the soured cream, mix well and spoon onto the salad. Toss ingredients until evenly coated, then season to taste with black pepper and salt. Serve with a sprinkled garnish of extra chopped chives if liked.

Note: For variation, try using the Italian garlic dressing (see page 132) instead of the soured cream and garlic mixture.

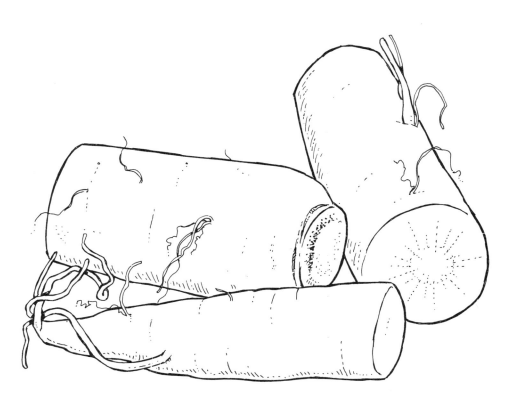

Lentil, Walnut and Bulgur Salad

Serves 6–8

4 oz (100g) continental
   lentils
1 small onion
2 whole cloves
1 bay leaf
1 teaspoon dried thyme
8 oz (225g) bulgur
   wheat
14 fl oz (400ml) boiling
   water
3 oz (75g) walnuts,
   chopped
1 red pepper, diced
1 bunch spring onions,
   chopped
2 tablespoons fresh
   parsley, finely
   chopped
Black pepper and salt

Dressing:

2 fl oz (50ml) red wine
   vinegar
6 fl oz (175ml) olive oil
2 cloves garlic, roughly
   chopped
1 level teaspoon ground
   fenugreek

Remove any grit or stones from the lentils and rinse well. Stick the cloves into the onion and place in a medium saucepan with the lentils, bay leaf and thyme. Add enough water to cover the lentils to about double their height, bring to the boil and then simmer for 20–25 minutes.

Meanwhile, put the bulgur wheat in a large bowl and pour in the boiling water. Stir briefly and leave to stand for 15–20 minutes, then fluff up with a fork.

While the lentils and bulgur wheat are softening, place all the dressing ingredients in a liquidizer and blend thoroughly. When the lentils are cooked, drain, remove the bay leaf and the clove-stuck onion, and add to the bulgur wheat.

Pour over the dressing while still warm, toss well and allow to cool a little. Then add the walnuts, red pepper, spring onions and parsley. Toss once more, season to taste and serve.

Avocado, Pear and Olive Salad

Serves 4-6

2 ripe avocados, halved, pitted, peeled and diced
2 fairly firm dessert pears (Packham or Williams are good), peeled and diced
4 oz (100g) mixed black and green olives, pitted and chopped, *or* 4 oz (100g) stuffed green olives, sliced into rings
1 quantity lemon and tarragon dressing (see page 127)

Reserve 2 or 3 of the chopped or sliced olives for garnish. Toss the prepared avocados and dessert pears in the dressing before any discolouration occurs. Add the olives and toss again. Sprinkle on the reserved chopped or sliced olives and serve.

Note: If serving this salad as a starter, try to keep the avocado shells intact after halving the fruits. Pile the salad back into the shells and serve with a salad garnish and a wedge of lemon. Alternatively, just pile a portion of salad on a large, fresh lettuce leaf placed on an individual serving plate, and arrange a few cucumber or tomato slices, or sprigs of watercress (or a combination of these) on one side of the salad, along with a lemon wedge if desired.

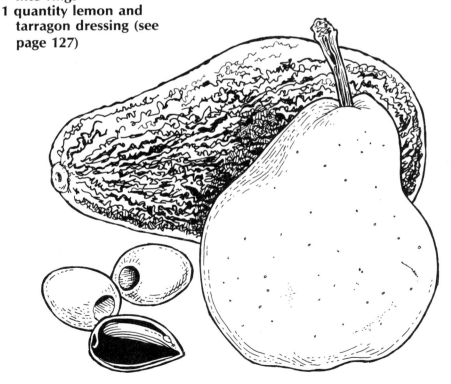

Potato-nut Salad

Serves 4–6

**1 lb (450g) potatoes
(preferably new
potatoes)**
**3–4 spring onions, *or* 2
tablespoons fresh
parsley *or* mint,
finely chopped**
**3 oz (75g) radishes,
sliced into rings, then
quartered**
**4 oz (100g) chopped
mixed nuts**
**4–5 tablespoons tofu
mayonnaise (see page
133)**
**2 teaspoons horseradish
(optional)**
Black pepper and salt

Scrub potatoes and boil until just tender. Drain, rinse in cold water and then stand in a saucepan of cold water for a few minutes to cool completely. Meanwhile, place the spring onions or herbs, radishes and nuts in a large bowl. Dice the cooked potatoes and add these to the mixture.

Beat the horseradish, if using, evenly into the mayonnaise, then spoon over the vegetables. Toss gently to coat all ingredients, season to taste and toss once more.

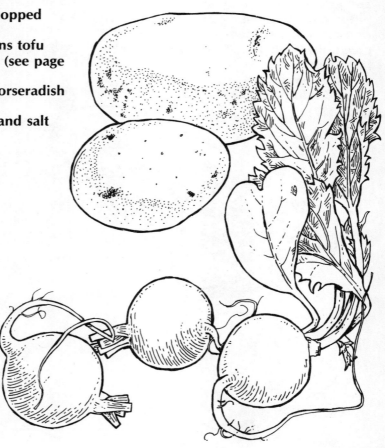

Cheesy Fennel Waldorf Salad

Serves 4-6

2 large dessert apples, diced
1 tablespoon freshly squeezed lemon juice
1 medium-large bulb fennel
3 sticks celery
2 oz (50g) walnut pieces
$\frac{1}{2}$ teaspoon celery seed
3 oz (75g) soynut cheese (see page 35) diced

Dressing:
4-5 tablespoons tofu mayonnaise (see page 133)
4-5 tablespoons soya yoghurt (see page 30)
A little black pepper and salt (optional)

In a large bowl, toss the diced apples in the lemon juice to prevent them from turning brown. Wash, trim and finely slice the fennel and celery sticks. Add to the apple together with the walnuts, celery seed and diced cheese. Mix the mayonnaise and yoghurt and pour over the salad. Toss the ingredients well together and season sparingly, if desired, with black pepper and salt.

Crisp Green and White Salad

Serves 4

1 small or ½ large Iceberg or Webbs lettuce

6 oz (175g) mange-touts, diagonally sliced

4 oz (100g) beansprouts

1 medium-large courgette, thinly sliced

1 bunch watercress, roughly chopped, *or* 3 oz (75g) alfalfa sprouts

5 oz (150g) mooli *or* kohlrabi, grated or cut into fine strips

1½ oz (37g) pumpkin seeds (optional)

1 quantity viniagrette dressing (see page 131)

Shred the lettuce and place in a large bowl with the mange-touts, beansprouts, courgette, watercress or alfalfa sprouts, mooli or kohlrabi, and the pumpkin seeds if using.

Pour the dressing over and toss all ingredients well together.

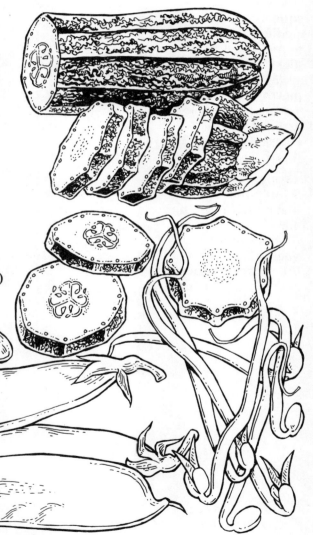

Celeriac and Sunflower Slaw

Serves 4-6

1½ oz (37g) sunflower
  seeds
½ teaspoon fennel seeds
  (optional)
1½ fl oz (40ml) white
  grape juice
8 oz (225g) white
  cabbage, shredded
6 oz (175g) carrots,
  grated or cut into
  thin julienne strips
6 oz (175g) celeriac,
  grated or cut into
  thin julienne strips
4 oz (100g) radishes, *or*
  3 oz (75g) dried
  apricots, cut into
  strips
7-8 tablespoons tofu
  mayonnaise (see page
  133)
1 teaspoon maple syrup
  or honey

Soak the sunflower seeds, and fennel seeds if using, in the grape juice for 1½-2 hours.

Put the prepared vegetables in a large bowl. Mix the mayonnaise with the syrup or honey. When the seeds have soaked, drain, reserving the juice, and add them to the salad. Whisk any remaining grape juice into the tofu dressing and spoon it over the salad. Toss all the ingredients well together and serve.

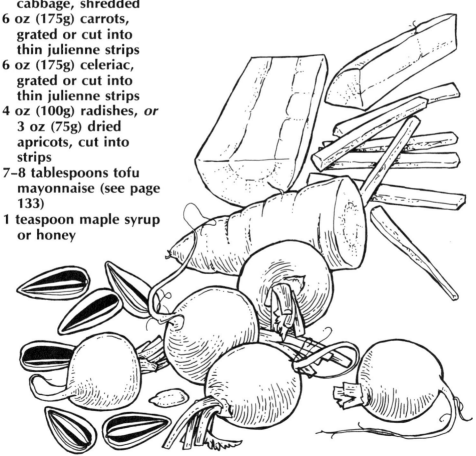

Aduki-coconut Salad

Serves 4–6

6 oz (175g) aduki beans
6–8 oz (175–225g)
   carrots, peeled and
   diced quite small
1½ oz (37g) shredded
   coconut
4–5 oz (100–150g) fresh
   figs, roughly
   chopped, *or* diced
   avocado, tossed in a
   little fresh lemon
   juice (optional)

Dressing:
1½ oz (37g) creamed
   coconut, grated
3 fl oz (75ml) hot water

Soak the aduki beans overnight or hot soak (see page 183). Rinse well and bring to the boil in about 1½ pints (850ml) water. Cover and simmer for about 40 minutes until just tender. Drain, rinse under a cold tap and place in a large bowl.

Using the same pan, place the carrots in just enough water to moisten its base and blanch them (covered) over a low/medium heat for 2–3 minutes. Allow to cool slightly and add to the aduki beans. Toss in the shredded coconut and either of the optional ingredients, if using.

Put the creamed coconut in a liquidizer goblet and add the hot water. Blend thoroughly and pour over the salad. Toss again and serve as it is or chilled.

SAUCES AND DRESSINGS

Quick Bechamel (White) Sauce

1 oz (25g) vegan
  margarine
1 rounded tablespoon
  fine-milled
  wholemeal flour
10–12 fl oz (275–350ml)
  soya milk
A pinch of ground bay
  leaves
A small pinch of
  nutmeg
Freshly ground black
  pepper and salt

Melt the margarine in a small/medium saucepan, add the flour and mix to a roux over a low heat. Add the soya milk a little at a time, stirring well after each addition to prevent lumps from forming and keep the sauce smooth. When $\frac{1}{2}$ pint (275ml) of milk has been added, stir in the ground bay leaves and nutmeg and increase heat. Continue stirring until the sauce has thickened. Then add a little more milk if a thinner consistency is desired, season to taste and serve.

Note: For extra flavour, heat the milk to near-boiling in a pan together with half an onion and leave to stand, covered, for 10 minutes before using. The onion can be saved and used in another dish.

Fines Herbes Sauce

½ oz (12g) vegan
  margarine
1 tablespoon finely
  chopped watercress
1 tablespoon finely
  chopped mustard and
  cress
1 tablespoon fresh
  parsley, *or* fennel
  tops *or* fresh basil,
  finely chopped
1 level tablespoon fine-
  milled, wholemeal
  flour
8–10 fl oz (225–275ml)
  concentrated soya
  milk
A pinch of nutmeg
  (optional)
Black pepper

Melt the margarine in a small/medium saucepan and gently cook the chopped herbs for 1–2 minutes. Stir in the flour to make a fairly thin roux. Gradually add the milk, stirring constantly to keep the sauce smooth. When all the milk has been added, increase the heat and stir until the sauce thickens slightly. Add up to ½ pint (275ml) milk, depending on consistency required. Taste, add a pinch of nutmeg and a little black pepper if desired, and serve.

Note: Other fresh herbs, such as mint, tarragon and sorrel, can also be tried to vary the flavour of this sauce.

Cheese Sauce

¾ pint (425ml) soya
  milk
3 oz (75g) vegan hard
  cheese (see page 35),
  grated
1 rounded tablespoon
  fine-milled,
  wholemeal flour
A good pinch each of
  mustard powder and
  paprika
Black pepper and salt

Blend half the milk with the grated cheese, flour and spices in a liquidizer. Heat the rest of the milk to near boiling and then pour into the liquidizer. Blend all ingredients thoroughly for at least 30 seconds, then return to the pan and heat, stirring constantly, until thickened. Season to taste with black pepper and salt.

Mushroom Cream Sauce

1 oz (25g) vegan
  margarine
3 oz (75g) mushrooms,
  wiped and finely
  chopped
1 dessertspoon sherry
6 fl oz (175ml) hot
  water
½ teaspoon Vecon*, *or*
  half a vegetable stock
  cube
1 oz (25g) fine-milled,
  wholemeal flour
1 teaspoon soya flour
6 fl oz (175ml) soya
  milk
Black pepper and salt

Melt the margarine in a medium saucepan and add the mushrooms. Cover and cook for 10–12 minutes until soft and juicy, adding the sherry for the last 3–4 minutes of cooking time. Dissolve the Vecon or half stock cube in the hot water and keep to one side. Sift the flours together and add to the cooked mushrooms, stirring briskly with a wooden spoon to form a roux. Keep the heat low and gradually add the soya milk, stirring all the time and ensuring that the flour is blended evenly (it should easily disengage from the mushroom pieces). When all the milk has been added, pour in the vegetable stock. Increase the heat and continue stirring until the sauce has thickened. Season to taste.

* Vecon is the name of a commercially-made stock concentrate, available from health-food stores and some supermarkets.

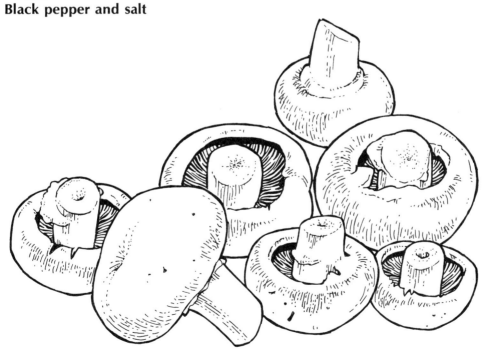

Savoury Brown Sauce

½ oz (12g) vegan margarine
1 tablespoon vegetable oil
1 onion, roughly chopped
2 oz (50g) mushrooms, thickly sliced or chopped
1 stick celery, sliced
1 medium carrot, roughly chopped
2 rounded teaspoons miso
¾ pint (425ml) hot water
1–2 teaspoons tamari (optional)

Heat the margarine and oil in a pan and stir in the prepared vegetables. Cover and cook over a gentle heat for 10–12 minutes. Dissolve the miso in the hot water and add to the pan. Bring to the boil and simmer on a low heat for 10 minutes. Allow to cool slightly, then liquidize and return to the pan. Taste, and add tamari if desired. Reheat to serve.

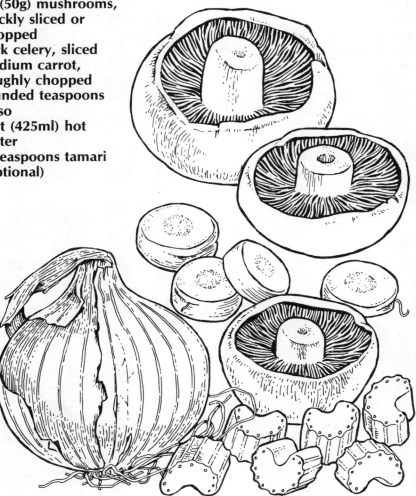

Almond and Rosemary Sauce

2 oz (50g) ground almonds
4 fl oz (100ml) soya milk
4 fl oz (100ml) vegetable stock, *or* 4 fl oz (100ml) water plus level teaspoon Vecon*
1 tablespoon sunflower oil
$\frac{1}{4}$ teaspoon dried rosemary, *or* $\frac{1}{2}$ teaspoon fresh chopped rosemary
1 level teaspoon oatbran and oatgerm mixture
A pinch of salt

Blend all the ingredients thoroughly in a liquidizer. Transfer to a saucepan and heat gently, stirring all the time, until thickened. Add a little more milk or water if a thinner consistency is preferred.

This sauce is pale and creamy with a subtle, delicious flavour. It can be used to pour over accompanying vegetables such as broccoli, as well as with stuffed courgettes (page 91). The sauce can be made richer or less rich by increasing the proportions of milk or water, respectively.

* Vecon is a commercially-made stock concentrate.

Tomato Sauce

1 small onion or $\frac{1}{2}$ large onion, roughly chopped
1 clove garlic, crushed
1 tablespoon olive oil
2 sticks celery, roughly chopped
1 teaspoon basil
1 bay leaf or $\frac{1}{4}$ teaspoon ground or cut bay leaves
1 × 14 oz (400g) tin tomatoes
1 tablespoon tomato purée
Black pepper and salt

Sauté the onion and garlic in the heated oil for 6–7 minutes. Add the celery, basil and bay leaf or leaves and continue to cook, covered, for a further 2–3 minutes. Stir in the tomatoes and tomato purée, bring gently to the boil and simmer for 15–20 minutes on a low heat. Season to taste with black pepper and salt.

Allow to cool slightly, then liquidize. Reheat before serving.

Curry Sauce

8 oz (225g) red lentils
2 tablespoons oil
1 clove garlic, crushed
   or finely chopped
1 teaspoon cumin seeds
1 teaspoon coriander
   seeds
$\frac{1}{2}$ teaspoon cardamon
   seeds
$\frac{1}{2}$ teaspoon mustard
   seeds
$\frac{1}{2}$ teaspoon turmeric
$\frac{1}{2}$ teaspoon chilli
   powder
1 teaspoon freshly
   grated root ginger
1 dessert apple, peeled
   and roughly chopped
1 pint (575ml) water
1 tablespoon freshly
   squeezed lemon juice

Pick over the lentils to remove any grit or stones and rinse thoroughly in a sieve. Leave to drain. Heat the oil in a medium-large saucepan and add the garlic, seeds, spices and ginger. Sauté over a low heat for 2–3 minutes, stirring occasionally. Add the drained lentils and apple, stir well and cook for a further minute or so. Pour in the water, bring to the boil and simmer gently for about 20 minutes, until the lentils are soft and most of the water has been absorbed. Stir in the lemon juice and beat with a wooden spoon to form a purée, then liquidize the mixture until smooth. More water can be added if a thinner consistency is desired.

Serve with mixed grain ring (page 92) or with a vegetable stir fry and warm wholemeal or pitta bread, or simply with a plate of freshly-cooked brown rice.

Mixed Grain Ring (page 92) with
Curry Sauce (page 128).

Courgette, Mushroom and Cheese Quiche
(page 106); Pepperoni Pizza (page 98).

Barbecue Sauce

1 tablespoon olive oil
1 onion, chopped
1 clove garlic, chopped
1 stick celery, roughly
  chopped
1 small carrot, roughly
  chopped
1 lb (450g) fresh, ripe
  tomatoes, skinned
  and chopped
2 tablespoons tomato
  purée
1 tablespoon soy sauce
1 tablespoon fresh,
  chopped parsley
2 teaspoons cider
  vinegar
1 thin slice of orange
1 tablespoon lemon
  juice
12 fl oz (350ml) apple
  or pineapple juice
A few drops of tabasco
  sauce (optional)
Black pepper and salt

Heat the oil in a medium saucepan and sauté the onion and garlic for 2–3 minutes until softened. Stir in the celery and carrot and cook for a further minute or two. Add the remaining ingredients, bring to the boil and simmer for 25–30 minutes. Remove from the heat and allow to cool slightly. Then liquidize the sauce and return it to the pan. Season to taste and reheat to serve.

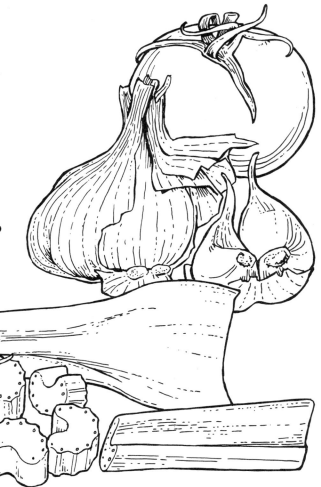

Hollandaise Sauce

8 oz (225g) silken tofu
4 tablespoons oil
 (preferably
 sunflower)
2 tablespoons lemon
 juice
2 teaspoons fresh,
 chopped tarragon, *or*
 1 teaspoon dried
 tarragon
1½ teaspoons soft
 brown sugar
Black pepper and salt

Blend all the ingredients in a liquidizer until smooth. This sauce can be served hot, but must not be boiled or simmered for any length of time.

Serve cold with avocado and pear starter(page 55), or hot with cooked vegetables such as Jerusalem artichokes or broccoli.

Tartare Sauce

1 × 10½ oz (300g)
 tetrapack of silken
 tofu
2 dessertspoons wine
 vinegar
1 tablespoon sunflower
 oil
1 tablespoon chopped
 capers
1 tablespoon chopped,
 fresh chives, *or* ½
 tablespoon dried
 chives, soaked for 30
 minutes in hot water
 and drained
Salt

Blend the first three ingredients in a liquidizer. Fold in the remaining ingredients and season to taste with a little salt.

Vinaigrette Dressing

2 fl oz (50ml) olive oil
2 tablespoons cider *or* white wine vinegar
1 teaspoon Dijon mustard
Black pepper and salt

Put all ingredients in a liquidizer, or in a jar or bottle with a screw-top lid, and liquidize or shake until well blended. If stored in the refrigerator before using, shake again or whisk with a fork before serving.

Lemon and Tarragon Dressing

3 fl oz (75ml) sunflower oil
Juice of half a lemon
3 teaspoons white wine vinegar
1 level teaspoon soft brown sugar *or* honey
2 teaspoons fresh, finely chopped tarragon, *or* 1 teaspoon dried tarragon

Blend all ingredients thoroughly in a liquidizer.

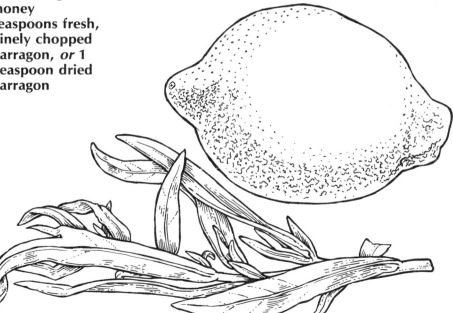

132   *Vegan Vitality*

Italian Garlic Dressing

5 tablespoons olive oil
2 tablespoons red wine
   vinegar
1 clove garlic, crushed
   or chopped
1 teaspoon finely
   chopped chives
1 teaspoon finely
   chopped red pepper
1 teaspoon fresh basil
   or marjoram, finely
   chopped
Black pepper and salt

Place the first three ingredients in a liquidizer and blend thoroughly until frothy. Add the remaining ingredients, give the dressing another *brief* whisk in the blender, and pour into a suitable jug or vessel to serve. If storing, cover and chill.

Thousand Island Dressing

1 × 10½ oz (300g)
   tetrapack of silken
   tofu
3 teaspoons tomato
   purée
2 tablespoons sunflower
   or safflower oil
1 tablespoon freshly
   squeezed lemon juice
3 teaspoons cider
   vinegar
3 tablespoons finely
   chopped red pepper
3 tablespoons finely
   chopped gherkin
1 tablespoon finely
   chopped fresh parsley
1 tablespoon chopped
   green olives
   (optional)
Black pepper and salt

Blend the first five ingredients in a liquidizer until smooth. Fold in the chopped red pepper, gherkin, parsley, and olives if using. Season to taste.

Tofu Mayonnaise

1 × 10½ oz (300g)
  tetrapack of silken
  tofu
2 tablespoons sunflower
  oil
1 tablespoon freshly
  squeezed lemon juice
3 teaspoons cider
  vinegar
1 teaspoon wholegrain,
  or yellow French *or*
  German mustard

Blend all ingredients in a liquidizer until smooth.
Store, chilled, in a screwtop jar or airtight
container.

Note: This mayonnaise can be varied by adding
a crushed clove of garlic, or fresh, chopped
herbs such as tarragon or chives.

VEGETABLES

Vegetable Mélange

Serves 4

6 oz (175g) parsnips
6 oz (175g) carrots
2 sticks celery
4 oz (100g) fine green beans
½ Chinese cabbage, shredded
1 oz (25g) vegan margarine
1 teaspoon ground fenugreek
2–3 oz (50–75g) dates, pitted and sliced
1 oz (25g) pecan nuts, halved or chopped (optional)
Black pepper and salt

Scrub or peel the parsnips and carrots. Cut them and the celery into julienne strips, and place them in a wok or large saucepan with the green beans and just enough water to cover the bottom. Cook for 5–7 minutes over a low-moderate heat until just becoming tender.

Add the Chinese cabbage and margarine. Toss gently in until the margarine has melted, then sprinkle over the fenugreek and add the dates. Cover and cook for a further minute or two, then carefully fold in the pecan nuts if using.

Season to taste and transfer to a warmed serving dish.

(The dates and fenugreek add an unusual mellow flavour to this vegetable stir-fry.)

Ginger-glazed carrots

Serves 4

1 lb (450g) carrots, cut into slender julienne sticks, 2–3 inches (5–8cm) long
$\frac{1}{2}$ oz (12g) vegan margarine
1 pinch of ground ginger
1 teaspoon maple syrup

Place carrots in a pan with 3 fl oz (75ml) water. Simmer, covered, for 8–10 minutes until beginning to soften. Add the margarine, ginger and maple syrup and cook uncovered for a further 2–3 minutes, gently tossing occasionally to coat the carrots evenly in the glaze.

Caribbean Potato Gratin

Serves 4–6

12 oz (350g) potatoes
12 oz (350g) sweet potatoes
1$\frac{1}{2}$ oz (37g) creamed coconut, grated
2 oz (50g) vegan hard cheese (see page 35) grated
4 fl oz (100g) soya milk
Black pepper and salt

Preheat the oven to 180°C (350°F, Gas 4). Peel and slice the potatoes and sweet potatoes thinly. Toss together the creamed coconut and cheese, and season sparingly with black pepper and salt.

Cover the base of a greased ovenproof dish with a layer of white potatoes and sprinkle over a little of the cheese and coconut mixture. Follow this with a layer of sweet potato slices sprinkled with the mixture. Repeat these alternate sprinkled layers, finishing with a top layer which shows alternating white and sweet potato slices around the edge and in the centre of the dish.

Pour the soya milk evenly over the slices, then top with the remainder of the grated mixture. Bake for 50–60 minutes until cooked through and toasted on top (a skewer can be inserted to test that the layers are tender through to the base).

Minted Courgettes and Mange-touts

Serves 4

8 oz (225g) courgettes, washed, topped and tailed, and sliced vertically
8 oz (225g) mange-touts, washed, topped and tailed
3 tablespoons cider *or* apple juice
½ teaspoon fresh, finely chopped mint, *or* ¼ teaspoon dried mint
½ oz (12g) vegan margarine
Freshly ground black pepper and salt

Place the courgettes and mange-touts in a pan with the cider or apple juice and mint and simmer, covered, for 5–7 minutes until just becoming tender. Add the margarine, stir in when melted and continue to cook, uncovered, until any excess liquid has evaporated to leave vegetables slightly crisp and covered with a glaze.

Season to taste with salt and pepper and transfer to a warmed serving dish.

Garnish with a sprig of fresh mint and serve.

Golden Potato and Onion Layer

Serves 4–6

1½ lb (675g) potatoes
2 medium-large onions, sliced into rings
1½ oz (37g) vegan margarine
A pinch of nutmeg
Black pepper and salt
A sprinkling of paprika or chopped parsley to garnish

Preheat the oven to 180°C (350°F, Gas 4). Peel or scrub and thinly slice the potatoes. Sauté the onions in 1 oz (25g) of the margarine until golden in colour. Lightly grease a 2-pint (1.25 litre) ovenproof dish and cover the bottom with a layer of potato slices. Cover this with a layer of onions, then season with black pepper and a very small sprinkling of nutmeg. Repeat the layers, seasoning after each and finishing with a layer of potatoes to either cover the top surface or form a ring around the edge of the dish.

Melt the remaining ½ oz (12g) margarine in a pan and brush the top layer of potatoes liberally with it. Bake for 60–80 minutes until the top layer of potatoes looks browned and golden.

Serve hot, as it is or garnished with a dusting of paprika or chopped parsley.

Swiss Chard with Water Chestnuts

Serves 4

1 lb (450g) Swiss chard
½ oz (12g) vegan
  margarine
1 teaspoon sunflower
  oil
1 medium onion,
  chopped
2 tablespoons sherry
1 tablespoon soy sauce
4 oz (100g) water-
  chestnuts
  (approximately 1
  small can) thinly
  sliced into circles
Black pepper and salt

Wash the chard thoroughly, trim off any tough parts at the base, and chop both leaves and stems (some people discard the stems, but I find that they add interest to the colour and texture of the cooked vegetable).

Melt the margarine with the oil in a large pan or wok and stir-fry the onion for a few minutes until softened. Add the chard, sherry and soy sauce and stir-fry for a further 2–3 minutes. Stir in the water chestnuts and cook for another minute, then season to taste and serve.

(Though chard is particularly good in this recipe, you can also use other leafy green vegetables such as savoy cabbage, spring greens or kale.)

Arame and Mushroom Stir-fry

Serves 4

1 oz (25g) dried arame
1 tablespoon vegetable
  oil
4 oz (100g) mushrooms,
  wiped and sliced
1 dessertspoon soy
  sauce
1 teaspoon grated fresh
  ginger
1 dessertspoon sherry
  (optional)
Black pepper and salt
  to taste

Soak the arame in a bowl or jug of warm water for 2–3 minutes until soft. Drain, reserving liquid for future use as a strong stock.

Heat the oil in a large frying pan or wok and add the mushrooms. Stir-fry for 2–3 minutes on a medium heat, then add the arame, soy sauce, ginger and sherry if using. Continue to stir-fry for another 5–7 minutes, adding a little reserved stock if necessary. Season to taste with black pepper and salt and serve.

This is delicious with rice and a simple tofu dish such as Tofu Foo-Yong (page 65), or just on its own with a few walnuts, cashews or almonds added and served on a bed of rice.

Brazilian Brussels Sprouts

Serves 4

1 lb (450g) Brussels
  sprouts, trimmed and
  washed
2 oz (50g) brazil nuts,
  roughly chopped
½ oz (12g) vegan
  margarine
Juice and finely grated
  rind of half a lemon
A pinch of nutmeg
Black pepper and salt

Place the brussels sprouts in a medium saucepan with just enough water to cover the base of the pan, and simmer over a medium heat for 8–10 minutes, until just becoming tender and the water has almost evaporated.

Meanwhile, spread the chopped brazil nuts on a baking sheet and place under a medium-hot grill for 5–8 minutes, turning occasionally to toast evenly. Then add the margarine to the sprouts along with the lemon juice, rind and nutmeg. Cook for a further 2–3 minutes, stir in the warm toasted brazil nuts, season to taste with black pepper and salt if desired, and turn onto a warmed serving dish to serve immediately.

Spiced Red Cabbage with Apple

Serves 4–6

1 tablespoon oil
2 dessert apples, cored
  and sliced vertically
1 level teaspoon
  cinnamon
1 level teaspoon
  coriander
½ medium-size red
  cabbage, finely
  shredded
¼ pint (150ml) cider *or*
  apple juice
2 oz (50g) chopped
  walnuts, *or* ½
  teaspoon caraway
  seeds
Black pepper and salt

Heat the oil in a pan and gently toss the apples and spices in it for 2–3 minutes. Add the cabbage and cider or apple juice, and simmer for 10–15 minutes until tender. Carefully stir in the walnuts or caraway seeds and season to taste.

Cauliflower in Mushroom and Chestnut Sauce

Serves 4

1 medium/large cauliflower
$\frac{1}{2}$ oz (12g) vegan margarine
3 oz (75g) mushrooms, roughly chopped
$\frac{1}{2}$ teaspoon dried tarragon, *or* 1 teaspoon fresh chopped tarragon
$\frac{1}{2}$ teaspoon dried rosemary, *or* 1 teaspoon fresh, chopped rosemary
$\frac{1}{4}$ pint (150ml) soya milk
3 fl oz (75ml) concentrated soya milk
6 oz (175g) tinned chestnut purée, mashed
$\frac{1}{2}$–1 tablespoon tamari (optional)
Black pepper and salt
A little concentrated soya milk and rosemary to garnish

Trim, wash and divide the cauliflower into florets. Place in a covered pan with just enough water to cover its base and simmer for 10–12 minutes until just tender, checking occasionally to add more water if necessary. Meanwhile, melt the margarine in a small saucepan and sauté the mushrooms with the herbs, covered, for 8–10 minutes. Stir in the soya milks and chestnut purée. Blend the mixture in a liquidizer until smooth, then return to pan, taste and add tamari and seasoning if desired. Reheat, stirring occasionally.

Drain the cooked cauliflower and place in a warmed casserole or serving dish. Pour over the sauce, garnish with a swirl of concentrated soya milk and a light sprinkling of rosemary, and serve.

(The sauce in this dish can be varied by omitting or including the tamari. Without it, a lighter colour and subtle, aromatic flavour is produced. With it, one obtains a more defined, richer taste and a slightly darker shade.)

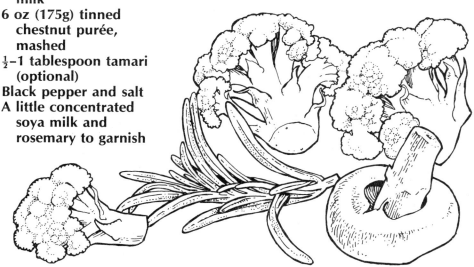

Ratatouille

Serves 4–6

1 large aubergine
3 tablespoons olive oil
1 large onion, sliced into rings
2 cloves garlic, crushed
2 medium-large courgettes, diagonally sliced
1 large or 2 small red *or* green peppers, sliced into rings
A good pinch of dried oregano
8 oz (225g) tomatoes, roughly chopped
¼ pint (150ml) tomato juice
1 tablespoon tomato purée
1 tablespoon freshly chopped parsley (optional)
Black pepper and salt

Top, tail and thickly dice the aubergine. Sprinkle the pieces with salt and leave to stand for 30 minutes, then rinse well and keep aside. Heat the oil in a large saucepan and sauté the onion and garlic for 4–5 minutes until softened. Add the aubergines, courgettes, peppers and oregano, cover and cook for a further 8–10 minutes over a low heat. Stir in the tomatoes, tomato juice and purée and simmer the mixture gently for 10–15 minutes, adding the parsley, if using, for the last 2–3 minutes of cooking time. Season to taste.

This can be served hot or as a salad.

Braised Chicory with Mushrooms and Tomatoes

Serves 4–6

2–3 heads chicory
  (about 12 oz or 350g)
Juice of half a lemon
1 quantity mushroom
  and tomato sauce
  (see page 83) omitting
  the parsley and bay
  leaf, and chopping or
  breaking up the
  tomatoes instead of
  liquidizing them

Preheat the oven to 180°C (350°F, Gas 4). Trim and rinse the heads of chicory and quarter them lengthways. Place in a large saucepan and pour over about ¾ pint (425ml) of water. Bring to the boil, then reduce heat, squeeze in the lemon juice and simmer for 6–8 minutes. Drain off the water (this will take with it much of the natural bitter taste of the chicory), and allow to cool slightly. Arrange the quarters in an ovenproof dish alongside each other, with cut surfaces facing upward and with bases and tops placed in alternate directions. Pour over the sauce, cover with foil or a lid and cook in the oven for 25–30 minutes.

Sesame Baked Parsnips

Serves 4

1 lb (450g) parsnips
2 teaspoons maple
  syrup
1 oz (25g) vegan
  margarine, melted
2 dessertspoons sesame
  seeds

Preheat the oven to 200°C (400°F, Gas 6). Peel the parsnips and cut them into shafts about 3–4 inches (7–10cm) by ½ inch (1cm) thick. Place in a large saucepan with the maple syrup and 2–3 fl oz (50–75ml) of water. Simmer, covered, over a moderate heat for 5 minutes, then drain off any excess water.

Pour most of the melted margarine into a warmed ovenproof dish, keeping back just a little for brushing the cooked vegetables. Add the sesame seeds and toss in the drained parsnips until coated and speckled with seeds. Bake for 30–40 minutes.

Remove from the oven, brush with the reserved melted margarine and serve.

PUDDINGS AND DESSERTS

Spiced Apple and Banana Crunch

Serves 6–8

1¼ lb (550g) eating apples
2 tablespoons freshly squeezed lemon juice
2–3 oz (50–75g) chopped, stoned dates (optional)
1 pinch of ground cloves
1 teaspoon ground cinnamon
3 bananas, sliced

Crumble topping:

2 oz (50g) plain, wholewheat flour
2 oz (50g) porridge oats
2 oz (50g) wheatgerm
2½ oz (62g) vegan margarine
2 oz (50g) brown sugar
2 oz (50g) chopped mixed nuts
½ teaspoon nutmeg
2 tablespoons sunflower oil

Preheat the oven to 180°C (350°F, Gas 4). Core and slice the apples either into rings or thin wedges. Toss gently in a saucepan containing the lemon juice and 4 tablespoons water. If using dates, add these, together with a further 3 fl oz (75ml) water. Simmer, covered, over a low heat for 8–10 minutes, until the apples are tender but not disintegrating. Fold in the spices, and the bananas, then turn the contents of the pan into a 2–2½ pint (1.25–1.5 litre) ovenproof dish and prepare the crumble topping.

Sift the flour into a large bowl and stir in the oats and wheatgerm. Rub in the margarine until the mixture resembles coarse breadcrumbs. Add the sugar, nuts and nutmeg, then pour the oil over and toss the ingredients well together. Sprinkle the crumble topping over the fruit and bake for about 25 minutes until golden.

Serve hot with a nut cream (see vegan dairy section), or apricot custard sauce (below).

Apricot Custard Sauce

3 oz (75g) dried apricots
¾ pint (425ml) soya milk
1 dessertspoon sugar

Chop the apricots into fairly small pieces and place in a saucepan with the milk and sugar. Bring gently to the boil, stirring, then simmer over a low heat for 2–3 minutes, stirring frequently. Cover, remove from the heat and leave for at least 30 minutes. Then liquidize the contents of the saucepan and return to the rinsed pan to reheat and serve (do not worry if the milk has a curdled appearance after soaking — final results are still superb!)

This sauce is delicious hot or cold over desserts, cakes, puddings, ice creams, or by itself.

Note: Alternatively, the sauce can be made by simmering the chopped apricots in 8 fl oz (225ml) water for 12–15 minutes, then liquidizing them with the sugar, returning to the pan, adding 8 fl oz (225ml) concentrated soya milk and reheating.

3-Tone Fresh Fruit Salad

Serves 4–6

2 dessert pears, peeled and diced

1 dessert apple, peeled and diced

2 bananas, diagonally sliced

2 dessertspoons freshly squeezed lemon juice

1 small or ½ a large honeydew melon

6 oz (175g) seedless green grapes

6 oz (175g) black grapes, halved and seeded

2–3 kiwi fruit, peeled and sliced into rings

2–3 tablespoons kirsch

3 fl oz (75ml) apple juice or clear grape juice

In a large bowl, gently toss the prepared pears, apple and bananas in the lemon juice. Use a melon-scoop to make balls of melon flesh and add these to the bowl together with the rest of the fruit. Mix the kirsch with the apple or grape juice and pour this over the salad. Toss gently again, cover and chill until ready to serve.

This is good on its own or with cashew or coconut pouring cream.

Note: Try varying the ingredients by substituting, for example, the pink flesh of guavas for the black grapes, or lychees for the melon balls.

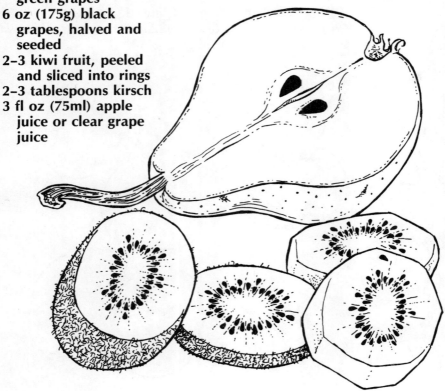

Om-ali Egyptian Cracked-wheat Pudding

Serves 4–6

4 oz (100g) cracked wheat
1½ pints (850ml) soya milk
½ oz (12g) vegan margarine
2 tablespoons maple syrup
1 teaspoon cinnamon
1 oz (25g) desiccated coconut, lightly toasted under grill
2 oz (50g) raisins
2 oz (50g) roasted hazelnuts, skinned and chopped or crushed
Freshly grated nutmeg

Preheat the oven to 170°C (325°F, Gas 3). Place all the ingredients except the nutmeg in a saucepan and bring gently to the boil. Simmer for 3–4 minutes, stirring occasionally. Transfer the mixture to an ovenproof dish, sprinkle with grated nutmeg and bake in the centre of the oven for 25–30 minutes.

Serve on its own or with a little pouring cream, in the form of concentrated soya milk or a nut or coconut cream (see The Vegan Dairy).

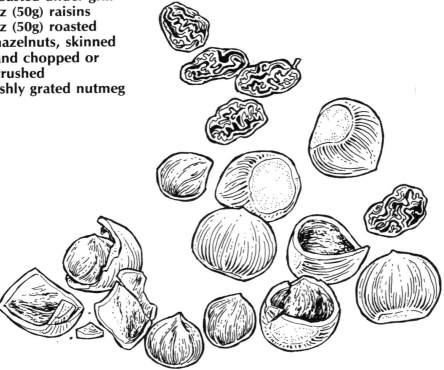

Apricot and Almond Supreme

Serves 4–6

6 oz (175g) dried apricots, roughly chopped

1 lb (450g) firm tofu, crumbled

4 tablespoons concentrated soya milk

2 fl oz (50ml) soya milk

1 rounded tablespoon maple syrup

2 tablespoons sunflower oil

3 oz (75g) ground almonds

Toasted, flaked almonds to garnish

Simmer the apricots in just enough water to cover them for 20–25 minutes until tender. Remove from heat and allow to cool slightly. Add the rest of the ingredients except the flaked almonds, mix well and blend in a liquidizer or food processor until smooth (if using a liquidizer, it might be easier to fold in the ground almonds after blending).

If a less firm consistency is desired, add a little more soya milk and blend again. Divide the mixture between 4–6 serving dishes or glasses, chill for 1–2 hours and serve with a sprinkling of toasted flaked almonds over each portion.

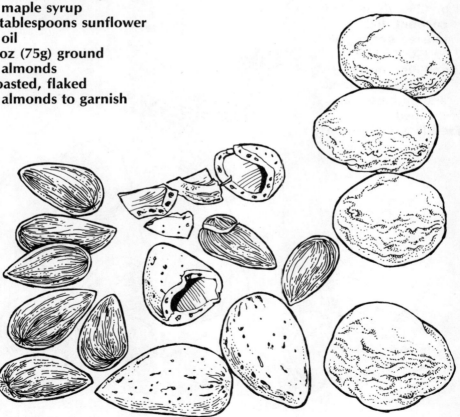

Mulled Fruit Salad

Serves 6

$\frac{3}{4}$ **pint (425ml) liquid**
(either $\frac{1}{4}$ pint/150ml
each of red wine,
apple juice and
ginger wine, *or* $\frac{3}{4}$
pint/425ml apple
juice)
1 cinnamon stick
2 whole cloves
4 oz (100g) dried
apricots, halved
(across the natural
'seam', leaving 2 flat
circles, if possible
4 oz (100g) prunes,
halved and pitted
4 oz (100g) dried figs,
quartered
1 oz (25g) raisins
2 large or 3 medium
oranges
1 oz (25g) flaked
almonds
1 piece stem ginger,
chopped (optional)
Extra flaked almonds to
garnish

Put the wines and/or apple juice into a large saucepan with the cinnamon stick, cloves, apricots, prunes and figs. Heat gently and simmer for 10–15 minutes until the fruit begins to swell and soften. Stir in the raisins and simmer for a further 2 minutes. Remove from heat and leave to soak overnight. Peel the oranges carefully with a sharp serrated knife to remove all covering pith. Slice into $\frac{1}{4}$-inch ($\frac{1}{2}$cm) thick circles, then cut these each into 6 wedges, removing any pith from the point of each wedge. Add the prepared orange to the soaked fruit with the flaked almonds and the stem ginger if using. Toss the ingredients gently together and serve, garnished with a few extra flaked almonds if desired.

This is a delicious idea for a winter fruit salad using dried and fresh fruit. Try varying the ingredients by using, for example, dried apples or peaches, or by using satsumas or tangerines instead of orange. For those concerned about using alcohol, don't forget that it loses its potency once cooked into a dish!

Note: This is equally good served hot or cold, on its own or with a vegan whipped or pouring cream (see vegan dairy section). It also goes well with a form of the cream-cheese topping on page 161, omitting the margarine and beating in enough freshly-squeezed orange juice to produce a soft 'whipped' consistency.

Strawberry and Hazelnut Cream Flan

Makes one 8-inch (20cm) flan

Base:
2½ oz (62g) vegan margarine
5 oz (150g) vegan digestive biscuits, crushed
3 oz (75g) hazelnuts, roasted, skinned and ground

Filling:
2 × 10½ oz (300g) tetrapacks silken tofu
2 punnets ripe, fresh strawberries, *or* 2 tins strawberries
1 banana peeled and sliced
3 oz (75g) soft brown sugar
1 teaspoon natural vanilla essence (optional)
2 teaspoons agar-agar
3 fl oz (75ml) juice from tinned strawberries, *or* apple juice, *or* water

First, prepare the base. Melt the margarine in a pan and add the crushed biscuits and hazelnuts. Mix thoroughly and press onto the base and sides of an 8-inch (20cm) flan tin. Chill in the refrigerator while preparing the filling.

Place the tofu in a large bowl, or food processor if available. If using fresh strawberries, rinse and keep 5 to one side for decoration. If using tinned strawberries drain and reserve 9 of the smaller ones.

Add the rest of the fruit to the tofu, together with the banana, sugar and vanilla essence if using. Mash the ingredients well together and liquidize in 2 or 3 batches (or purée in one batch if using a food processor).

Heat the juice or water and agar-agar together in a small saucepan, stirring constantly, until boiling. Remove from heat, cool slightly, then stir briskly into the filling mixture. Pour into the prepared base and chill the flan for about 3 hours until firm.

Use the reserved strawberries to decorate the top (if using fresh strawberries, cut each in half before arranging them around the edge; if using tinned strawberries, arrange 8 around the edge and place the ninth in the centre).

Serve on its own or with whipped cream (see page 32).

Maple-ginger Cheesecake

Serves 8-10

Base:
3 oz (75g) vegan
   margarine
5 oz (150g) vegan
   digestive biscuits
1 rounded tablespoon
   fine or pinhead
   oatmeal
1 rounded tablespoon
   wheatgerm
1 teaspoon cinnamon
$\frac{1}{2}$ teaspoon ground
   ginger

Filling:
1 lb (450g) firm tofu,
   crumbled
4 rounded tablespoons
   maple syrup
3 tablespoons sunflower
   oil
3-4 pieces stem ginger,
   chopped
1 or 2 extra pieces of
   stem ginger, thinly
   sliced, to garnish

Preheat the oven to 180°C (350°F, Gas 4). To make the base, melt the margarine in a pan and add the crushed biscuits, oatmeal, wheatgerm and spices. Mix well and press firmly into the base of an ungreased, loose-bottomed 8-inch (20cm) cake tin. Place in refrigerator while preparing the filling.

Place the tofu in a food processor if available, or in a large bowl. Add the maple syrup and oil, and blend or mash thoroughly (use an electric whisk if no blender or processor is at hand). Fold in the chopped ginger and spread this filling evenly on top of the base.

Bake in the middle of the oven for 35-40 minutes until just beginning to brown a little on the surface.

Remove from the oven and allow to cool in the tin for 10-15 minutes. Then slide off the side-section of the cake tin and leave to cool completely on a wire rack. Garnish with thin slices of stem ginger.

Carob and Orange Cheesecake

Serves 8–10

- 6 oz (175g) vegan digestive biscuits, crushed
- 3 oz (75g) vegan hard margarine
- 1 orange
- 1 lb (450g) firm tofu
- 4 oz (100g) soft brown sugar
- 2 oz (50g) carob powder
- 4 tablespoons sunflower oil
- 1 small block of plain chocolate (optional, for garnish)

Preheat the oven to 180°C (350°F, Gas 4). Melt the margarine in a pan and stir in the biscuit crumbs. Mix well and press into the base of an 8-inch (20cm) loose-bottomed cake tin. Chill in the refrigerator while preparing the filling.

Peel the orange with a potato-peeler and grind the rind finely in a grinder. Then squeeze the juice from the peeled orange and reserve.

In a large bowl, mash together the tofu, sugar, carob powder, oil, orange rind and juice. Mix well, preferably finishing the mixing in a blender or liquidizer for a creamier texture.

Pour the mixture onto the prepared base and bake in the middle of the oven for 35–40 minutes. Allow the cheesecake to cool in the tin before removing. When cool, you can decorate the top of the cake with chocolate curls, using a potato-peeler to peel curls from a block of chocolate.

Serve on its own or with one of the creams on pages 33–34 (cashew nut cream is particularly good with this cake).

Crème Caramel

Serves 6–8

- 3 oz (75g) white granulated *or* caster sugar
- 3 tablespoons water
- 1 lb (450g) firm tofu, *or* 12 oz (350g) firm tofu plus 4 oz (100g) silken tofu
- 3 tablespoons sunflower *or* corn oil
- 3 tablespoons maple syrup
- 1 teaspoon natural vanilla essence

(I have made an exception in this dish by using a little white sugar for a successful caramel.)

Preheat the oven to 180°C (350°F, Gas 4). Gently heat the sugar and water in a saucepan, stirring constantly with a metal spoon, until the sugar has dissolved. Then keep bubbling on a steady boil, without stirring, until the colour turns to a rich brown caramel (take care not to let the mixture turn too dark or it will taste bitter). Remove from the heat, add 1 teaspoon of boiling water and pour into a 1½–2 pint (1 litre) ovenproof dish or mould. Tilt the dish a little to coat the base evenly and then leave to set.

Meanwhile, prepare the 'crème'. Blend the tofu together with the maple syrup, oil and vanilla essence until smooth and creamy, using a liquidizer, food processor or electric mixer.

When the caramel is completely cool, pour the tofu mixture on top, smooth the surface, with the back of a spoon and place the dish in a roasting pan containing about a 1-inch (2.5cm) depth of freshly boiled water. Cook in the centre of the oven for 50–55 minutes until slightly browned on top.

Remove the dish from the roasting pan and allow to cool. When ready to serve, run a knife around the edge of the dish, place a serving plate on top and invert.

Peach Crème Brûlée

Serves 4–6

8–10 oz (225–275g) fresh *or* canned peaches
8 oz (225g) firm tofu, crumbled
1½ tablespoons maple syrup
1½ tablespoons concentrated soya milk
1 teaspoon natural vanilla essence (optional)

Topping:
1–1½ oz (25–37g) soft brown *or* caster sugar

If using fresh peaches, peel and remove the stones. If using the canned variety, drain and rinse under cold water. Roughly chop the peaches and put in a liquidizer or food processor with the rest of the ingredients except for the sugar topping. Blend until smooth and creamy.

Spoon into individual ramekin dishes and sprinkle the sugar as evenly as possible over the surface of each one (caster sugar will result in a crunchy, toffee-like coating, whereas brown sugar will melt to form a shiny coating, but will not crystallize). Place the dishes under a medium-hot grill for 5 minutes until the sugar has melted and, if using caster sugar, caramelized. Allow to cool, then chill for at least 1½ hours before serving.

Chocolate-chestnut Fudge Dessert

Serves 4

7 oz (1 × 200g bar) plain eating chocolate
5 tablespoons concentrated soya milk
4 tablespoons maple syrup
3–4 tablespoons brandy or rum, *or* 4 tablespoons apple or orange juice plus a few drops of natural vanilla essence if available
10 oz (275g) tinned chestnut purée, mashed
Extra concentrated soya milk or other pouring cream (see vegan dairy section), plus a little grated chocolate

Place chocolate, milk, syrup and liqueur or fruit juice in a medium saucepan, together with vanilla essence if using, and heat over a larger saucepan containing simmering water. Stir until ingredients are well blended.

Add the mashed chestnut purée, mix well and then beat until smooth (a puréeing device can be used if available, to produce an extra smooth and even consistency). Spoon mixture into 4 individual ramekins and chill for at least 45 minutes. When ready to serve, pour over a little extra concentrated soya milk or other pouring cream, such as cashew nut (page 33) or coconut (page 34), and sprinkle on a little extra grated chocolate.

Date and Banana Ice-cream

8 oz (225g) dates
1 pint (575ml) water
1 vanilla pod
6 tablespoons vegetable oil
4 oz (100g) soya-milk powder
3 bananas, peeled and sliced

Place the dates, water and vanilla pod in a pan, bring gently to the boil, cover and simmer for 15–20 minutes until very soft.

Allow to cool a little, then remove vanilla pod and transfer to a liquidizer goblet or food processor. Add the remaining ingredients and blend until smooth and creamy.

Either freeze in an electric ice-cream maker or transfer to a plastic container and freeze for several hours before serving.

Strawberry-coconut Yoghurt Ice-cream

1 × 10 oz (275g) can,
  or 1 punnet ripe,
  fresh strawberries
¾ pint (425ml) thick
  soya yoghurt (see
  page 36)
1 banana, sliced
2 tablespoons maple
  syrup (or honey if
  eaten)
4 fl oz (100ml) juice
  from can, *or* apple
  juice, *or* water
1½ teaspoons agar-agar
  flakes
1 oz (25g) creamed
  coconut, grated

Drain the canned strawberries, reserving 4 fl oz (100ml) of the juice, or, if using fresh strawberries, rinse them under a cold tap. Place strawberries, yoghurt, banana and syrup or honey in a food processor or liquidizer. Blend thoroughly. Put the measured juice or water in a small saucepan with the agar-agar and creamed coconut and heat gently, stirring, till it begins to boil. Reduce heat and simmer, still stirring, for 2–3 minutes. Remove from heat, allow to cool slightly (only 2–3 minutes or the agar-agar will begin to set), then pour into the yoghurt mixture and blend all ingredients well together until smooth and creamy. Transfer to a suitable container and freeze for at least 4 hours before serving.

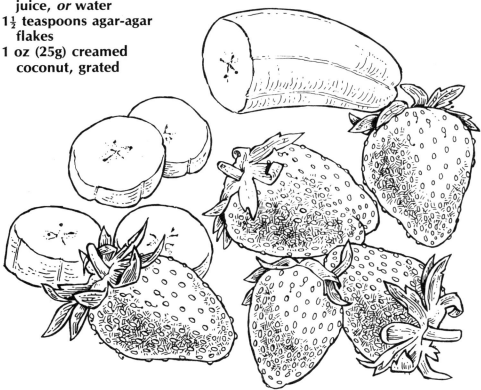

Highland Ambrosia

Serves 4–6

1½ oz (37g) fine/medium oatmeal

1½ oz (37g) ground almonds

1 oz (25g) nibbed almonds

2 level dessertspoons wheatgerm

8 oz (225g) firm tofu

¼ pint (150ml) concentrated soya milk

1 tablespoon freshly squeezed lemon juice

3 tablespoons maple syrup

3 tablespoons whisky, *or* 3 tablespoons orange juice

Finely grated rind of 1 lemon

Thin slices of lemon to garnish

Mix the oatmeal, almonds and wheatgerm together and spread evenly on a baking tray. Toast under a medium grill, turning frequently, for a few minutes until slightly browned. Transfer to a mixing bowl and leave to cool.

Meanwhile, place the tofu with all the remaining ingredients in a liquidizer and blend until smooth. Pour over the cooled dry ingredients and mix thoroughly. Cover and chill the mixture for at least 1 hour (during this time some of the liquid will be absorbed and the consistency will become thicker). Pile into individual serving glasses and garnish each portion with a twist of lemon.

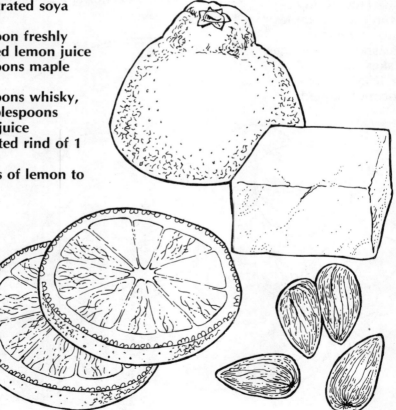

Creamy Pumpkin and Pecan Pie

Makes one 8-inch (20cm) pie

Base:

4 oz (100g) plain, wholemeal flour

1 dessertspoon soya flour

2 oz (50g) medium *or* coarse oatmeal

1 tablespoon wheatgerm

3 oz (75g) vegan margarine

1 oz (25g) brown sugar

Filling:

10 oz (275g) firm tofu, mashed

10 oz (275g) cooked and drained pumpkin flesh, roughly chopped

4 tablespoons sunflower *or* corn oil

1 tablespoon molasses

2½ oz (62g) light soft brown sugar

1 teaspoon cinnamon

½ teaspoon ground ginger

½ teaspoon nutmeg

3 oz (75g) sultanas

3 oz (75g) pecan nuts, chopped

8 pecan halves to decorate

Preheat the oven to 180°C (350°F, Gas 4). To make the pie shell, sift the flours together and stir in the oatmeal and wheatgerm. Cream the margarine and sugar until light and fluffy, then gradually fold in the flour mixture and beat until well blended. Press onto the sides and base of a greased 8-inch (20cm) sponge or flan tin and bake for 10–12 mintues until firm. Leave to cool on a wire rack while preparing filling.

Reset the oven to 170°C (325°F, Gas 3). Blend all the filling ingredients, except the nuts, in a food processor or liquidizer (the mixture will have to be blended in 3 or 4 batches if a liquidizer is used). Fold in the chopped pecan nuts and pour the filling into the cooled flan case. Smooth the surface with the back of a spoon and bake for 30–40 minutes until set.

Allow to cool for about 10 minutes before decorating with 8 pecan halves gently pressed into the surface of the pie around its edge.

Serve on its own, with cashew nut cream (see page 33) or concentrated soya milk. (This pie also makes a popular picnic dessert.)

CAKES AND BISCUITS

Almond and Poppy Seed Cake

Makes one 7–8 inch (17–20cm) round cake

3 oz (75g) poppy seeds
4 fl oz (100g) soya milk
5 oz (150g) vegan margarine
5 oz (150g) soft brown sugar
5 oz (150g) silken tofu, drained
6 oz (175g) plain, fine-milled, wholemeal flour
1 oz (25g) soya flour
3 rounded teaspoons baking powder
½ teaspoon bicarbonate of soda
3 oz (75g) ground almonds

Preheat the oven to 180°C (350°F, Gas 4). Put the poppy seeds and milk in a small pan and bring gently to the boil. Remove from heat, cover and leave to stand for about half an hour.

Meanwhile, cream the margarine with the sugar until light and fluffy. Add the tofu and beat in well, preferably with an electric hand whisk.

Sift the flours, baking powder and bicarbonate of soda together and stir in the ground almonds.

Fold the soaked poppy seeds with any remaining milk into the creamed mixture. Then fold in the flour and almond mixture, half at a time, and beat thoroughly for a minute or so to blend the ingredients well and produce a soft, firm consistency. Turn into a greased 7–8 inch (17–20cm) round cake tin and bake in the centre of the oven for 40 minutes. Then turn the setting down to 170°C (325°F, Gas 3) for a further 30–35 minutes. The cake is cooked when the centre feels firm and slightly springy to the touch, or when a fine skewer inserted through the middle comes out clean.

Carob Fudge-truffles

Makes 9 oz (250g) truffles

6 oz (175g) dates, chopped
8 tablespoons water
1 oz (25g) vegan margarine (preferably not softspread)
1 tablespoon malt extract
1 teaspoon rum (optional)
1 oz (25g) carob powder
1 oz (25g) soya-milk powder
Carob powder, *or* grated non-dairy carob bar, to coat

Place the dates and water in a small pan and heat to a simmer. Cover and cook over a low heat for 6–8 minutes, until the dates are very soft and most of the water has been absorbed. Empty the contents into a sieve and, holding the sieve over the same pan, rub the date-pulp through to remove and discard any coarse pieces of skin or stones. Add the margarine and malt extract to the sieved purée in the pan and heat gently until melted and blended. Then add the rum if using, and the carob and soya-milk powders. Beat all the ingredients well together, allow to cool, then cover and chill in the refrigerator for 2 hours.

After this time, scoop out small amounts of the mixture with a melon baller or teaspoon. Roll each piece into a ball and coat in the carob powder or grated carob. (If using carob powder, roll the coated truffle between the palms of your hands briefly to remove any excess of powder and leave a thin, even coating.)

Peanut Health Candy

Makes 10–11 oz (275–300g)

4 oz (100g) peanut butter
4 tablespoons maple syrup *or* honey
2 oz (50g) sunflower seeds
2 oz (50g) sesame seeds
1 oz (25g) desiccated coconut
1 oz (25g) raisins (optional)

Gently heat the peanut butter and syrup or honey together in a pan. Stir well to blend them evenly, then mix in the remaining ingredients. Press the mixture into a suitable container (preferably square or rectangular) and allow to cool completely. Cover and chill in the refrigerator for 1 hour, then cut into squares.

Carob Crumb Cake

Makes one 8-inch (20cm) cake

2½ oz (62g) vegan
  margarine
1 oz (25g) soft brown
  sugar
3 tablespoons soya milk
6 oz (175g) digestive
  biscuits, crushed
1 oz (25g) carob
  powder
3 oz (75g) cake crumbs
2 oz (50g) raisins
1 oz (25g) walnuts,
  crushed or chopped

Topping:

4 oz (100g) plain
  chocolate *or* carob
  bar
2 tablespoons soya milk

Gently heat the first 3 ingredients in a saucepan until the margarine has melted. Meanwhile, mix the remaining ingredients together in a bowl.

Add the biscuit mixture, one-third at a time, to the saucepan, stirring well after each addition. Press into a loose-bottomed 8-inch (20cm) round cake tin and put into the refrigerator to set. Then remove the sides of the tin and transfer the cake to a serving plate.

To make the topping, heat the carob or chocolate with the soya milk, 'bain-marie' style in a pan or bowl over a saucepan of simmering water. Blend well together till smooth and spread evenly over the top of the cake. Allow the topping to cool and set before serving.

Apricot Fruit Cake

Makes one 8-inch (20cm) cake

3 oz (75g) sultanas
3 oz (75g) currants
3 oz (75g) dried apricots, roughly chopped
3 oz (75g) dates, roughly chopped
8 fl oz (225ml) apple juice
7 oz (200g) plain, fine-milled wholemeal flour
1 oz (25g) soya flour
1 rounded teaspoon bicarbonate of soda
1 teaspoon mixed spice
3 oz (75g) brown sugar
4 fl oz (100ml) sunflower *or* corn oil
Juice of half a lemon
2 tablespoons apricot jam (preferably sugar-free)

Using a large mixing bowl, soak the fruit overnight in the apple juice. Preheat the oven to 170°C (325°F, Gas 3). Sift the flours together with the bicarbonate of soda and mixed spice. Stir the sugar into the soaked fruit, then mix in the oil, lemon juice and apricot jam. Add the flour mixture and beat well for about a minute. Pour into a greased 8-inch (20cm) cake tin and bake for 55–60 minutes. To test that the cake is cooked through, insert a thin skewer through the centre and check that it comes out clean.

You can also use dried or tinned pineapple as an alternative to apricots.

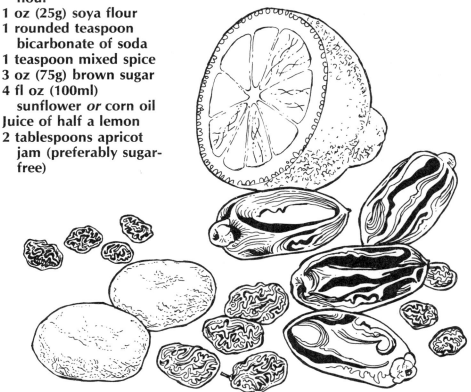

Tofu, Prune and Lemon Cake

Makes one 9½–10 inch (24–25cm) ring-cake

8 oz (225g) prunes, stoned and roughly chopped
¼ pint (150ml) water
10 oz (275g) fine milled, wholemeal plain flour
2 level teaspoons bicarbonate of soda
6 oz (175g) silken tofu
Juice and finely grated rind of 1 lemon
6 oz (175g) soft brown sugar
4 fl oz (100ml) sunflower oil

Coconut frosting:
4 oz (100g) creamed coconut, grated
Finely grated rind of half a lemon
1 tablespoon maple syrup
3 fl oz (75ml) hot water
1 tablespoon freshly squeezed lemon juice
2 dessertspoons desiccated coconut, lightly toasted

Preheat the oven to 180°F (350°C, Gas 4). Put the prunes and water in a covered pan, bring to the boil and simmer gently for 10–15 minutes until tender. Then remove the lid and continue to cook over a low heat until most of the water has evaporated or been absorbed. Remove from the heat and set aside to cool slightly. Sift the flour together with the bicarbonate of soda into a mixing bowl.

Place the tofu in a liquidizer, food processor or separate mixing bowl with the lemon rind and juice, sugar and oil. Blend until smooth and creamy (using an electric hand whisk if other equipment is not available).

Add the flour to the tofu mixture half at a time, beating thoroughly and briskly after each addition. Lastly, fold in the cooked prunes. Spoon the mixture into a greased 9½–10 inch (24–25cm) ring tin and bake for 35–40 minutes. Leave in tin for 5 minutes after removing from oven before turning out to cool on a wire rack.

To prepare the frosting, place the grated creamed coconut in a liquidizer with the lemon rind and maple syrup. Pour in the hot water and blend well until light and creamy. Add the lemon juice and blend again. Allow to cool for a few minutes, then spoon it carefully over the cake, using the back of the spoon to coax the mixture to 'flow' down the sides of the cake a little.

Sprinkle with a little toasted, desiccated coconut for a final decorative finish.

Minted Courgettes and Mange-touts
(page 136); Ginger-glazed Carrots (page 135);
Spiced Red Cabbage with Apple (page 138);
Swiss Chard with Chestnuts (page 137).

Apricot Fruit Cake (page 159) with Cashew
Nut Cream (page 33); Strawberry and
Hazelnut-Cream Flan (page 148).

Carrot and Banana Cake

Makes one 8-inch (20cm) cake

8 oz (225g) plain, fine-milled wholemeal flour
2 level teaspoons baking powder
2 teaspoons cinnamon
8 oz (225g) carrots, peeled and grated
2 oz (50g) pecan nuts or walnuts, chopped
3 oz (75g) vegan margarine
2 tablespoons corn oil
3 oz (75g) brown sugar
4 tablespoons maple syrup *or* honey
2 bananas mashed
1–2 tablespoons soya milk
Extra chopped pecan nuts *or* walnuts to decorate

Frosting:
3 oz (75g) cream cheese (see page 36)
½ oz (12g) vegan soft margarine
2 tablespoons maple syrup *or* honey
1 teaspoon freshly squeezed lemon juice

Preheat the oven to 170°C (325°F, Gas 3). Sift the flour with the baking powder and cinnamon into a large mixing bowl. Toss in the grated carrots until evenly coated, and add the nuts. Gently heat the margarine, oil, sugar, and syrup or honey in a pan until melted together, then mix in the mashed bananas. Pour the contents of the pan into the bowl and mix all the ingredients thoroughly. Add enough of the soya milk to produce a moist dropping consistency, beat well and spoon the mixture into a greased 8-inch (20cm) cake tin. Bake for 65–75 minutes in the centre of the oven, until the cake feels firm and slightly springy when pressed in the centre. Cool in the tin for 4–5 minutes, then turn out to cool completely on a wire rack.

To make the frosting, cream the soft cheese and margarine, preferably with an electric whisk, until light and fluffy. Add the syrup or honey and continue beating to a smooth, even texture. Finally, add the lemon juice, beat well in and spread the mixture over the top of the cooled cake. Sprinkle with a few chopped nuts to finish.

Orange and Oat Cake

Makes one 8-inch (20cm) round or square cake

3 oz (75g) plain fine-milled wholemeal flour

1 rounded tablespoon soya flour

2 teaspoons baking powder

¾ teaspoon nutmeg

6 oz (175g) fine/medium oatmeal *or* porridge oats

1 oz (25g) wheatgerm

3 oz (75g) soft brown sugar

3 fl oz (75ml) soya milk

2 fl oz (50ml) water

4 tablespoons vegetable oil

Juice and finely grated rind of 1 orange

1 heaped tablespoon marmalade (preferably the reduced sugar type)

Orange frosting:

1 oz (25g) vegan margarine

2½ oz (62g) soft brown sugar

Juice and finely grated rind of half an orange

Sprinkling of toasted, chopped mixed nuts (optional)

Preheat the oven to 180°C (350°F, Gas 4). Sift the flours, baking powder and nutmeg together and mix with the oats, wheatgerm and sugar in a large bowl.

Combine the milk, water, oil, orange rind and juice in a measuring jug and stir these into the dry ingredients, beating well to produce a moist, smooth, but fairly firm consistency. Finally, fold in the marmalade. Spoon the mixture into a greased 8-inch (20cm) round or square cake tin and bake for 35–40 minutes in the centre of the oven, until the top of cake is firm to the touch and a skewer comes out clean when inserted into its centre.

Leave in the tin for 5–10 minutes before turning out to cool on a wire rack.

To make the frosting, beat the margarine, sugar and orange rind together until creamy, then gradually add the juice, beating well after each addition, until a light, fluffy texture is achieved. Spread this over the top of the cake and sprinkle with toasted chopped mixed nuts for an attractive finish.

Malted Carob Brownies

Makes 12 brownies

6 oz (175g) dried dates, chopped
¼ pint (150ml) water
1 rounded tablespoon malt extract
3 oz (75g) vegan margarine
3½ oz (87g) wholemeal self-raising flour
1½ oz (37g) carob powder
1–2 tablespoons soya milk
2 oz (50g) chopped walnuts

Topping:
2 oz (50g) vegan margarine
4 tablespoons concentrated soya milk
2 tablespoons carob powder
2 oz (50g) brown sugar

Preheat the oven to 180°C (350°F, Gas 4). Place the dates in a small pan with the water and simmer for 20–25 minutes until very soft, stirring occasionally to help break up the fruit. Add the malt extract and mash well to a purée. Beat in the margarine and leave to cool slightly. Sift the flour and carob powder together and fold into the date mixture. Add a tablespoon of the soya milk and mix thoroughly. If the mixture seems a little stiff, add another tablespoon of milk. Finally, fold in the walnuts. Spread the mixture in a greased 7-inch (18cm) shallow, square baking tin. Bake for 25–30 minutes until firm. Allow to cool in the tin, then cut into squares and ice with the topping.

To make the topping, place all the ingredients in a small pan and heat gently, stirring constantly until bubbling. Reduce heat and continue stirring for 1–2 minutes, then remove from the heat. Beat the mixture as it cools until it thickens, then chill in the refrigerator for 20–30 minutes. Beat again and spread on the top of each brownie.

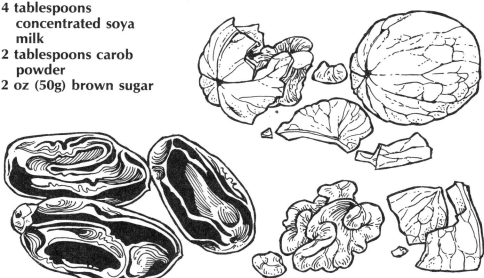

Blackcurrant and Hazelnut Slices

Makes 12–15 slices

2 punnets fresh
    blackcurrants, *or* 2 ×
    10½ oz (300g) cans
    blackcurrants
1–2 tablespoons maple
    syrup *or* honey
6 oz (175g) fine milled,
    wholemeal flour
6 oz (175g) porridge
    oats
5 oz (150g) vegan
    margarine
2 oz (50g) soft brown
    sugar
5 oz (150g) hazelnuts,
    toasted, skinned and
    finely crushed or
    ground

Preheat the oven to 190°C (375°F, Gas 5). If using fresh blackcurrants, rinse thoroughly and simmer for 10 minutes in just enough water to cover the bottom of the pan (about 2 tablespoons). Then add 2 tablespoons maple syrup or honey and mash well. If using canned blackcurrants, drain off the liquid and mash with one tablespoon syrup or honey. Keep the prepared fruit to one side. Sift the flour into a bowl and mix with the oats. Rub in the margarine until the mixture resembles coarse breadcrumbs, then stir in the sugar and hazelnuts evenly.

Press half of the oat-nut mixture firmly into the base of a greased 8-inch (20cm) square baking tin. Cover with the blackcurrants, then sprinkle on the remaining oat-nut mixture and press this down quite firmly, using the back of a spoon to press and smooth the surface. Bake for 30–35 minutes. Allow to cool completely in the tin, then cut into slices.

Peanut Butter Biscuits

Makes about 18 biscuits

6 oz (175g) fine-milled
    wholemeal flour
2 level dessertspoons
    wheatgerm
3½ oz (87g) vegan
    margarine
3 oz (75g) soft brown
    sugar
2 heaped tablespoons
    peanut butter

Preheat the oven to 180°C (350°F, Gas 4). Sift the flour and stir in wheatgerm. Cut the margarine into small pieces and rub into the flour with the fingers until the texture resembles that of coarse breadcrumbs. Stir in the sugar. Add the peanut butter and mix in well with a fork until a firm, evenly blended dough is obtained.

Roll out on a lightly floured surface and cut into squares or fingers, or use a biscuit cutter to ensure a more 'professional' finish.

Place the shapes on lightly oiled or greased baking sheets and bake for 15–20 minutes.

Allow the biscuits to cool on the tray for 2–3 minutes before transferring to a wire rack.

These biscuits keep well in an airtight container.

Digestive Biscuits

Makes about 24 biscuits

7 oz (200g) fine-milled, wholemeal flour
½ teaspoon salt
1 slightly rounded teaspoon baking powder
1½ oz (37g) fine oatmeal
4 oz (100g) vegan margarine
2 oz (50g) soft brown sugar
2 tablespoons soya milk

Preheat the oven to 180°C (350°F, Gas 4). Sift the flour into a mixing bowl with the salt and baking powder, and stir in the oatmeal. Rub in the margarine until the texture resembles that of breadcrumbs. Stir in the sugar, then add enough of the soya milk to produce a soft dough. Roll out on a lightly floured surface until quite thin (a little less than ¼ inch (5mm) thickness) and cut with a round biscuit cutter. Place on lightly greased baking sheets and bake for 15–20 minutes until firm and golden. Use a metal spatula to transfer carefully to a wire rack to cool.

Choc-nut Crunches

Makes 15–16 biscuits

4 oz (100g) vegan margarine
3 oz (75g) soft brown sugar
5 oz (150g) plain, wholemeal flour
1 level teaspoon baking powder
3 oz (75g) hazelnuts, toasted, skinned and crushed *or* chopped
3 oz (75g) chipped plain chocolate *or* chopped, non-dairy carob bar

Preheat the oven to 180°C (350°F, Gas 4). Cream the margarine and sugar until light and smooth. Sift the flour and baking powder together and gradually fold into the butter and sugar mixture. Beat well, then fold in the hazelnuts and chocolate or carob chips. Roll the resultant dough into balls about 1 inch (2.5cm) in diameter, place on a lightly oiled baking tray and press down a little on the tops to flatten them slightly, leaving ¾–1 inch (2–2.5cm) space between the pieces. Bake in the upper part of the oven for 15–20 minutes, until golden brown.

Aniseed and Orange Cookies

Makes 20–24 cookies

4 oz (100g) vegan margarine
3 oz (75g) soft brown sugar
Juice and finely grated rind of 1 medium orange
8 oz (225g) fine-milled, wholemeal flour
2 rounded teaspoons ground aniseed

Preheat the oven to 180°C (350°F, Gas 4). Beat margarine, sugar and orange rind together until light and fluffy. Gradually add the orange juice, beating well after each addition (do not worry if the mixture appears to curdle at this stage, as this should not affect the final results).

Sift flour and aniseed together and fold, half at a time, into the sugar and margarine mixture. Beat well until the ingredients are thoroughly blended and the texture is smooth and even.

Drop mixture, a rounded teaspoonful at a time, onto lightly greased baking sheets. Leave about 1 inch (2.5cm) between each shape. (You can pipe them through a cream bag and nozzle to make neater shapes or designs.)

Bake for 10–15 minutes, until just turning a golden colour. Cool on a wire rack.

Orange Marzipan

Makes 14–15 oz (400–425g) marzipan

6 oz (175g) ground almonds
2 oz (50g) soya flour
6 oz (175g) soft brown sugar
2–3 tablespoons freshly squeezed orange juice
Finely grated rind of half an orange, *or* 1 teaspoon natural vanilla *or* natural almond essence *or* 1–2 teaspoons brandy

Put the ground almonds in a mixing bowl and stir in the sifted soya flour and sugar. Mix in enough of the orange juice to form a stiff dough-like consistency and knead well for a minute or two. Add any of the optional ingredients, mix well in with a fork and knead again briefly.

This is one of my more indulgent recipes (to make it even more so, substitute a little brandy, cointreau or other liqueur for some of the orange juice!). It is a super mixture to use for cakes, to fill fresh dates as part of a buffet or an after-dinner accompaniment to coffee, or to shape into petits fours. It is also the base for one of the fillings for the Scandinavian Supper Ring (see page 175).

BREADS AND QUICKBREADS

Wheaten Soda Bread

Makes one 2 lb (900g) round loaf

- 1¼ lb (550g) fine-milled, wholemeal flour
- 2 teaspoons bicarbonate of soda
- 3 teaspoons cream of tartar
- 1 level teaspoon salt
- 4 oz (100g) fine oatmeal
- 8 fl oz (225ml) soya milk
- 1 tablespoon sunflower oil
- 6–7 fl oz (175–200ml) cold water

Preheat the oven to 220°C (425°F, Gas 7). Sift the flour, bicarbonate of soda, cream of tartar and salt together in a large bowl. Stir in the oatmeal. Make a well in the centre and pour in the milk, oil, and enough of the water to mix the ingredients to a soft (but not sticky) dough. Knead briefly and firmly on a floured surface, then shape into a round about 1½ inches (4cm) thick. Mark it into 4 fardels by cutting a deep cross on the top of the round, making sure that the 4 edges of the cross cut approximately ½ inch (1cm) into the sides of the loaf from top to base.

Bake in the centre of the oven for 30 minutes, then transfer to a wire rack to cool.

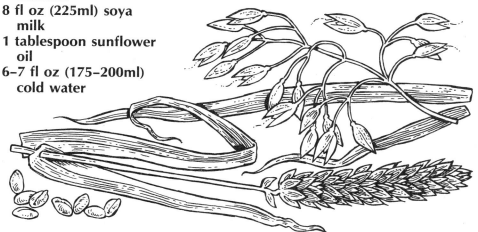

Wholewheat Bread

***Makes 2 × 1 lb (450g)
loaves***

1½ lb (675g) wholemeal
  flour
1 rounded teaspoon
  soya flour
1½ teaspoons salt
¾–1 pint (425–575ml)
  warm water (⅓
  boiling, plus ⅔ cold
  water)
1 tablespoon malt
  extract
1 oz (25g) fresh yeast
1 tablespoon oil
2 tablespoons cracked
  wheat
Extra oil for brushing

Sift the flours and salt into a large mixing bowl. Measure out ¼ pint (150ml) freshly boiled water and dissolve the malt extract in it. Then make the solution up to ¾ pint (425ml) by adding cold water. Crumble in the yeast, mix well and leave to stand in a warm place for about 10 minutes until the top becomes frothy. Make a well in the centre of the flour mixture and add the yeast solution with the oil, mixing with a wooden spoon or spatula until a dough begins to form. Knead the dough in the bowl for 8–10 minutes, adding a little more warm water if necessary to produce a texture which is smooth and elastic.

Leave in the bowl and cover with a sheet of oiled cling-film or a warm, damp tea cloth and put in a warm place to allow the dough to rise to approximately double its size. This will take 1½–2 hours.

Then punch the dough down to release the air and knead again for a further 5–6 minutes. If making loaves, divide into 2 pieces and place in 2 greased 1 lb (500g) loaf tins. If making rolls, divide into pieces each about 3 oz (75g) in weight. Shape these and place them on greased baking sheets, leaving space between them for expansion. Return to a warm place for 35–45 minutes until again doubled in size, then brush with a little extra oil, sprinkle with cracked wheat and bake at 200°C (425°F, Gas 7) for 35–40 minutes if making loaves, or 17–20 minutes if making rolls. The bread is cooked when a hollow sound can be heard if the base of the loaves or rolls is tapped with the knuckles.

After removing from oven, turn out onto a wire rack to cool.

Note: This recipe can also be used to make pitta bread. Simply knead and roll the dough out flat after it has doubled in size instead of shaping into rolls or loaves. Then cut it into circles about 4–5 inches (10–13cm) across. Roll these briefly to elongate them into oval shapes, then cook under a medium/hot grill for 3–4 minutes on each side.

Quick Sunflower-seed Bread

Makes one large and one small loaf

- **18 fl oz (500ml) warm water (6 fl oz/175ml boiling water and 12 fl oz/350ml cold water)**
- **1 oz (25g) fresh yeast**
- **1 rounded teaspoon molasses *or* 1 level teaspoon raw sugar**
- **1 lb (450g) wholemeal flour**
- **1 level teaspoon salt**
- **4 dessertspoons sunflower seeds**

In a large bowl, mix the water with the yeast and molasses or sugar, and leave in a warm place for about 5 minutes. Meanwhile, sift the flour and salt together and stir in the sunflower seeds.

Gradually add the flour mixture to the yeast mixture and beat with an electric mixer on low speed for about 2 minutes.

Divide between lightly greased 2 lb (1 kg) and 1 lb (500g) loaf tins. Place these in the centre of a cold oven. Set heat to 250°C (490°F, Gas 9) and bake for 25 minutes. Then reduce heat to 200°C (400°F, Gas 6) and bake for a further 25 minutes.

Remove from the oven and transfer to a wire rack to cool.

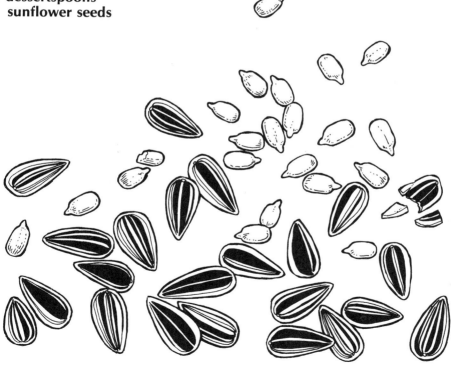

Malted Mixed Grain Bread

Makes approximately 2 × 1 lb (450g) loaves

1 oz (25g) wheat grains *or* cracked wheat

1 oz (25g) rye grains *or* cracked rye

3 fl oz (75ml) apple juice

1 lb (450g) fine-milled wholemeal flour

4 oz (100g) barley flour

1½ teaspoons salt

2 oz (50g) rye flakes

2 oz (50g) millet flakes

1 tablespoon malt extract

¾ pint (425ml) warm water (approximately)

1 oz (25g) fresh yeast

1 tablespoon vegetable oil

Rinse and soak the whole or cracked grains overnight in the apple juice.

Sift the flours and salt into a large bowl and stir in the rye and millet flakes.

Drain the grains, reserving the juice, and add these to the flour mixture.

Dissolve the malt extract in ¼ pint (150ml) freshly boiled water, then add the reserved apple juice and make the liquid up to ¾ pint (425ml) with cold water. Crumble in the yeast, stir briefly and leave to stand in a warm place for about 5 minutes.

Make a well in the flour mixture and pour in the yeast solution and the oil, mix well with a wooden spoon and then knead on a floured surface for 7–8 minutes. Return to the bowl, cover with a warm damp cloth or oiled cling-film and leave the dough to stand in a warm place for 15–20 minutes. Knead again in the bowl for 2–3 minutes, then either shape the dough into one large or two small round or cottage loaves, or divide it between two 1 lb loaf tins. Cover the loaves again and leave in a warm place for 1–1¼ hours until doubled in size, then bake for 35–40 minutes in a hot, 220°C (425°F, Gas 7) oven until golden brown and sounding hollow when tapped on their bases.

Turn out of the tins and allow to cool on a wire rack.

Rye-oat Bread with Caraway and Fennel Seeds

Makes 4 oval 1 lb (450g) loaves

1½ lb (675g) wholemeal flour
1 dessertspoon caraway seeds
1 dessertspoon fennel seeds
1 heaped teaspoon molasses
1½ pints (850ml) warm water
2 oz (50g) fresh yeast
1 lb (450g) rye flour, sifted
8 oz (225g) coarse oatmeal *or* porridge oats
3 teaspoons salt
3 tablespoons oil

Sift the wholewheat flour and stir in the seeds. Dissolve the molasses in the warm water and mix in the yeast. Add the wholemeal flour and seeds and beat well to a smooth, even batter. Cover with oiled cling-film or a warm damp cloth and leave in a warm place for about 1 hour, until well risen.

Add the remaining ingredients and mix well together with a wooden spoon to form a dough. Knead in the bowl for 4–5 minutes, then divide into 4 pieces. Shape into oval loaves and place on lightly oiled baking trays. Use a blunt knife to mark with fairly deep ($\frac{1}{4}$–$\frac{1}{2}$ inch/5–10mm) diagonal cuts about 1 inch (2.5cm) apart across the top of the loaves. Cover as before and return to a warm place for 50–60 minutes, until doubled in size. Meanwhile, preheat the oven to 220°C (425°F, Gas 7). Bake the loaves for 35–40 minutes.

Sesame Corn Bread

Makes 2 × 1 lb (450g) loaves

1 teaspoon brown sugar
¾ pint (425ml) warm water
1 oz (25g) fresh yeast
1 lb (450g) wholewheat flour, sifted
8 oz (225g) cornmeal
2½ oz (62g) sesame seeds
1½ teaspoons salt
1 tablespoon sunflower oil
Extra sesame seeds to decorate

Dissolve the sugar in the warm water and mix in the yeast. Add 12 oz (350g) of the wholemeal flour and beat thoroughly until a smooth batter is obtained. Leave to stand in a warm place, covered with oiled cling-film or a warm damp cloth, for 1 hour.

Mix the remaining 4 oz (100g) of wholewheat flour with the cornmeal, sesame seeds and salt. Add these to the risen batter, together with the oil, and mix well with a wooden spoon until a dough forms. Knead for 7–8 minutes until smooth, then divide into two pieces and place in lightly oiled 1 lb (500g) loaf tins. Sprinkle the tops of the loaves with sesame seeds and gently press them into the surface. Cover again and leave in a warm place for 50–60 minutes, until doubled in size. Meanwhile, preheat the oven to 220°C (425°F, Gas 7). Bake the loaves for 30–35 minutes until they look golden and sound hollow when tapped on the base. Turn out onto a wire rack to cool.

Fig and Ginger Brack

Makes one 2 lb (900g) loaf

- 8 oz (225g) dried figs, chopped
- ½ pint (275ml) strong herb tea, such as 2 bags orange blossom, linden blossom or camomile
- 8 oz (225g) wholemeal self-raising flour
- 2 teaspoons baking powder
- 3 oz (75g) brown sugar
- 2 tablespoons sunflower *or* corn oil
- 3-4 pieces stem ginger, finely chopped, plus 1 tablespoon of their syrup, *or* 2 tablespoons ginger conserve

Immerse the figs in the herb tea while still very hot and leave to stand for 2–3 hours or overnight.

Preheat the oven to 180°C (350°F, Gas 4). Sift the flour and baking powder together and stir in the sugar.

When the figs have soaked, add the oil, ginger and syrup (or ginger conserve). Stir and pour into the flour mixture. Beat well for 2–3 minutes to blend ingredients thoroughly, then pour into a greased 2 lb (1 kg) loaf tin and bake for 50–60 minutes until risen and firm to the touch.

Cool in the tin for 5–7 minutes, then turn out and place on a wire rack to cool completely.

Serve sliced, with margarine if desired.

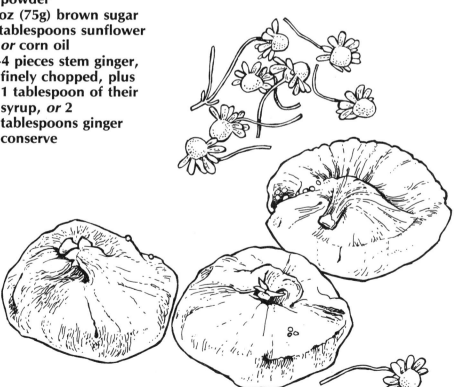

Rich Scandinavian Supper Ring

Makes one ring

Enriched dough:
8 oz (225g) fine-milled, wholemeal flour
1 rounded tablespoon soya flour
1 rounded tablespoon barley flour
A pinch of salt
1 dessertspoon soft brown sugar
½ oz (12g) fresh yeast
4 fl oz (100ml) lukewarm soya milk
2 oz (50g) vegan margarine
Soya milk or oil for brushing
Sesame seeds, *or* flaked almonds, *or* poppy seeds to garnish

A succulent and attractively different alternative to sandwiches and cakes at tea and supper time. I have given one sweet and one savoury option for fillings here, but use your imagination to make many others!

Sift the flours and salt into a large bowl and stir in the sugar. Cream the yeast with a little of the milk, then gradually stir in the rest of the milk and leave to stand in a warm place for 5–7 minutes. Melt 1½ oz (37g) of the margarine and add this, together with the yeast and milk, to the flour mixture. Mix well with a wooden spoon to form a dough, then knead in the bowl for 7–8 minutes. Cover with oiled cling-film or a warm, damp cloth and put in a warm place for 1–1¼ hours until doubled in size.

Meanwhile, prepare the filling (see below). Preheat the oven to 200°C (400°F, Gas 6). Knead the risen dough for a further 2–3 minutes, then roll it out on a floured surface to form an oblong about 4 × 10 inches (10 × 25cm). Spread half the remaining margarine (or scatter small pieces of it if it is hard) over the surface of the dough. Fold the top third of the oblong over the centre and the bottom third over these to form a smaller rectangle. Rotate this 90° so that the longer sides are vertical, then roll again to the original size and shape and repeat the process. Wrap the dough in cling-film and refrigerate for about 20 minutes. After this time, repeat the above procedure, without using any more margarine, 3 more times. Finally, roll out to make an oblong approximately 7 × 14 inches (18 × 36cm). Spread the prepared filling over the dough and roll it up from the long side to form a pipe-like shape. Carefully bend this into a ring, place on a lightly greased baking tray, and join the two ends of the ring together by gently pressing and pinching. Use a sharp pointed knife to make deep slanting cuts around the outside edge of the ring, about 1 inch (2.5cm) apart.

Brush the top of the ring with a little soya milk or oil and sprinkle on the seeds or nuts. Cover again with oiled cling-film or a warm damp cloth and leave in a warm place to rise for 30–40 minutes. Bake for 30 minutes.

Superb served warm or cold!

Filling 1: Celery, Cheese and Raisin
3 oz (75g) finely chopped celery
3 oz (75g) vegan hard cheese (see page 35), grated
3 oz (75g) raisins, chopped or minced
Warm water to mix
1 oz (25g) poppy seeds (optional)

Mix all ingredients together (a food processor would be handy here to chop and mix the first 3 ingredients at once to a fine, grainy texture). Add enough warm water to produce a soft but quite firm spreading consistency. Season to taste if desired.

Filling 2: Almond and Cinnamon
1 quantity orange marzipan (see page 166)
2–3 tablespoons freshly squeezed orange juice
$\frac{1}{2}$–1 teaspoon ground cinnamon (to taste)

Add enough of the orange juice to the marzipan to produce a soft (but not sloppy) spreading consistency. Mix in the ground cinnamon to taste.

Raisin, Bran and Wheatgerm Muffins

Makes 10–12 muffins

- 5 oz (150g) fine-milled wholemeal flour
- 1 tablespoon soya flour
- 2 level teaspoons baking powder
- 1 oz (25g) wheatgerm
- 1 heaped tablespoon bran
- 1 oz (25g) soft brown sugar
- 2 oz (50g) raisins
- 3 tablespoons sunflower oil
- ¼ pint (150ml) cold water

(These are delicious as they are, but for variation try adding, for example, a stick of finely chopped celery, a fresh grated apple, or a few dried apricots, soaked and chopped, to the mixture.)

Preheat the oven to 190°C (375°F, Gas 5). Sift the flours with the baking powder into a bowl and stir in the wheatgerm, bran, sugar and raisins. Add the oil and water and mix well to form a fairly stiff but moist batter. Spoon into greased bun or muffin tins and bake for about 25 minutes. Leave in the tins for 4–5 minutes after removing from oven, then turn out and serve while still warm or allow to cool completely on a wire rack.

This is good with herbed or otherwise flavoured cream or soft cheeses; with sweet spreads; or just with margarine.

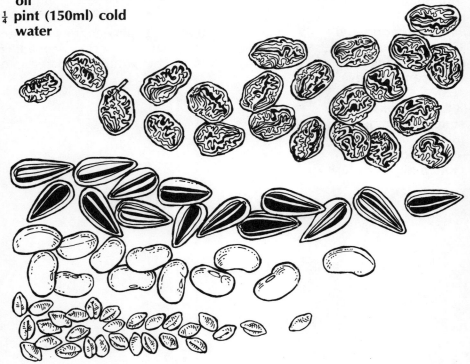

Cheese and Herb Scones

Makes 10 × 2½-inch (6cm) scones

- **8 oz (225g) plain, fine-milled wholemeal flour**
- **1 tablespoon baking powder**
- **A pinch of salt**
- **2 oz (50g) vegan margarine**
- **A good pinch each of dried sage and thyme, *or* ¼ teaspoon each of fresh, finely chopped sage and thyme**
- **3 oz (75g) grated vegan cheese (see page 35)**
- **5 fl oz (150ml) soya milk**
- **Extra grated cheese for sprinkling**

Preheat the oven to 220°C (425°F, Gas 7). Sift the flour, baking powder and salt together in a bowl. Rub in the margarine until a breadcrumb-like texture is achieved. Stir in the herbs and grated cheese. Mix enough of the soya milk in to produce a soft, quite moist (but not sticky) dough. Knead this lightly and roll it out on a floured surface to a thickness of about ¾ inch (2cm). Cut with a 2½-inch (6cm) dough cutter and place on a lightly oiled baking sheet.

Brush the tops of the scones with any remaining soya milk and sprinkle over a little extra grated cheese. Bake for 10–15 minutes, until the scones are risen and the topping is melted and golden.

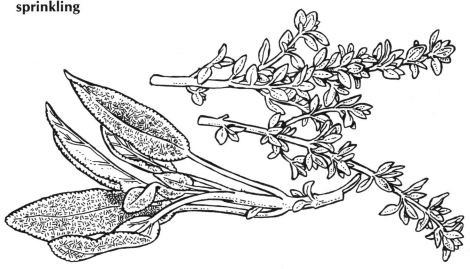

Mexican Tortillas

Makes 14–15 tortillas

5 oz (150g) cornmeal
6 fl oz (175ml) freshly boiled hot water
1 tablespoon oil
7 oz (200g) plain, fine-milled wholemeal flour
1 level teaspoon salt
1½ oz (37g) vegan margarine

Mix the cornmeal with the hot water and oil to form a stiff paste. Leave to stand for 7–8 minutes. Sift the flour and salt together in a large bowl and rub in the margarine. Add the cornmeal paste and mix well with a wooden spoon. Knead the resultant dough for a few minutes until soft and even-textured. Divide into about 14 pieces, rolling each into a ball. Roll out each ball on a floured surface to form a circle of about 6–8 inches (15–20cm) diameter. Cook in an ungreased frying pan over a medium heat for 3–4 minutes on each side, until their light colour is speckled with darker spots.

Pile on a warm serving dish and cover with foil until needed.

Serve with chilli con coconut (page 66), or fill with the aduki-bean tacos mixture (page 68) and accompany with a crunchy side salad.

Note: A little oil added to the frying pan will make the tortillas crisper. These are good with pâtés or dips at a buffet, or with starters such as guacamole (page 57).

INSTRUCTIONS FOR MAKING SOYA MILK AND TOFU

Makes over 1 lb (450g) tofu or approximately 3 pints (1.75 litres) soya milk

12 oz (350g) soya beans, soaked overnight
3 pints (1.75 litres) hot water
2 level teaspoons nigari*, *or* 2 teaspoons magnesium sulphate*, *or* 5 tablespoons cider vinegar, *or* 5 tablespoons freshly squeezed lemon juice } (these are all curdling agents)

Stage 1: Soya milk

Rinse the soaked beans thoroughly in a colander and place 4 oz (100g) at a time in a liquidizer with 1 pint (575ml) of the hot water. Blend thoroughly. Pour all the liquidized beans into a large saucepan and bring gently to the boil, stirring constantly. Reduce heat to a low simmer for about 15 minutes, stirring frequently to prevent any sticking of the ground beans on the bottom of the pan. Meanwhile, line the colander with muslin (preferably two thicknesses), and set it over a large pan or bowl. Gradually ladle in the contents of the pan. The soya milk will drain through into the bowl. After 2–3 minutes, pick up the corners of the muslin and twist together in order to apply more pressure to the remaining contents and release as much soya milk as possible. The residue of pulp left in the muslin is sometimes referred to as 'okara'. It is high in fibre and contains some protein, B vitamins and potassium, and can be reserved, if desired, for use in cakes, casseroles and so on (see page 188).

Stage 2: Tofu
Return the soya milk to the rinsed saucepan, bring gently to the boil again and simmer for 4–5 minutes, stirring frequently. Mix the curdling agent with $\frac{1}{4}$ pint (150ml) hot water (if using nigari or magnesium sulphate, make sure these are dissolved). Stir this solution into the soya milk briefly, then cover and leave for 5–7 minutes to curdle.

Line the colander (or suitably sized plastic container with holes pierced in it to allow the whey to drain through) with two fresh layers of muslin and set it over a large pan or bowl. Ladle in the curdled soya milk. The tofu will be caught in the muslin, while the whey is strained out and can either be discarded or used as an alternative stock for soups and other savoury dishes. When most of the liquid has drained through, fold the muslin over the top of the tofu and place a weight (a plate with a heavy jar or two on it will do) on top to press it into a firm, solid shape. Leave for 15–20 minutes, then carefully unwrap and turn out the tofu.

If not using immediately, store the tofu by submerging it in cold water in a plastic container. It will then keep for 3–4 days in the refrigerator, if the water is changed every day.

* *nigari* is a substance extracted from sea water. It comprises the crystallized minerals which are left behind when the water and salt are removed.

magnesium sulphate is more commonly known as Epsom salts!

Quick Home-made Tofu

Makes approximately 8 oz (225g) tofu

6 oz (175g) soya flour
3 pints (1.75 litres) water
1½ tablespoons cider vinegar, *or* freshly squeezed lemon juice

Sift the flour into a large saucepan and gradually pour in the water, mixing to a paste at first to avoid the formation of lumps. Leave to soak for 50–60 minutes. Then bring gently to the boil, stirring constantly, and simmer for 20–25 minutes over a low heat, giving a frequent stir to prevent sticking at the bottom of the pan. Add the cider vinegar or lemon juice, stir round the pan once or twice and leave for 7–10 minutes. Set a colander lined with muslin over a large bowl and ladle in the curds and whey which will have formed in the pan. When most of the whey has passed through into the bowl, bring the edges of the muslin together, wind round and squeeze down on the tofu gently to remove more whey. Empty the bowl and replace the colander, placing a weight (such as a plate holding a heavy jar) on top. Leave for at least 3–4 hours. Remove the tofu from the muslin and store in the refrigerator, immersed in a container of water. It will keep for 4–5 days if water is changed daily.

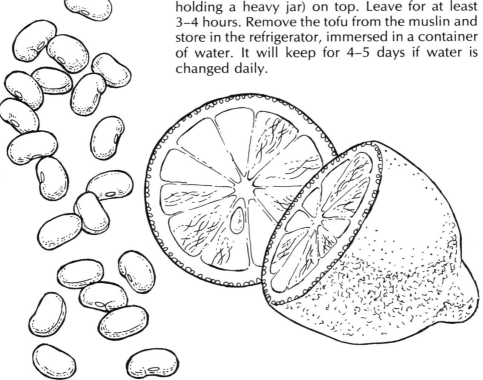

KITCHEN TIPS AND INFORMATION

The Soaking and Cooking of Pulses and Grains

After picking over your chosen pulses for any foreign matter such as grit or small pieces of stalk, rinse them thoroughly to remove any remaining dust before soaking.

The following charts show which pulses and whole-grains actually need to be soaked, and for how long they then need to be cooked. If you are using a pressure-cooker you will need to reduce the stated cooking-times by two-thirds (for example, if the stated cooking time is 60 minutes, pressure-cook for only 20 minutes).

Do *not* add salt either to cooking or to soaking water, as this will tend to toughen the outer skins of the pulse or grain and prolong cooking time. If anything, add a small piece of kombu (a sea-vegetable) to help make the beans, peas and/or grains more easily digestible. Use plenty of water (about 4 times the volume of the ingredient, or double its height in the saucepan) in which to cook the grains or pulses, and keep any leftover stock for future use in casseroles, soups and so on. Do not forget, incidentally, that both leftover stock and any cooked beans not immediately needed can be frozen without adversely affecting their texture or flavour.

Cold soak
This simply means soaking the pulses or grains in double their height of cold water for 7–12 hours, or overnight.

Hot soak
Place the grains or pulses in a saucepan, cover to double their height in water, bring to the boil, cover and simmer for 3–4 minutes. Switch off heat and leave to stand for 1 hour.

Soaking and Cooking Chart

GRAIN OR PULSE	SOAK NEEDED (if 'yes', choose *cold* or *hot* soak above)	COOKING TIME
ADUKI BEAN	YES	40–50 minutes
BARLEY GRAIN	NO	50–60 minutes
BLACK BEAN	YES	60 minutes
BLACK-EYED BEAN	YES	35–40 minutes
BROAD BEAN	YES	80–90 minutes
BUCKWHEAT GRAIN	NO	17–20 minutes
BUTTER BEAN	YES	50–60 minutes
CANNELLINI BEAN	YES	50–60 minutes
CHICK PEA	YES	60–80 minutes
CORN GRAIN*	NO	8–10 minutes
FIELD BEAN	YES	40–50 minutes
FLAGEOLET BEAN	YES	40–50 minutes
HARICOT BEAN	YES	50–60 minutes
LENTIL — CONTINENTAL	NO	35–45 minutes
LENTIL — GREEN	NO	35–45 minutes
LENTIL — PUY	NO	35–45 minutes
LENTIL — RED	NO	15–25 minutes
MILLET GRAIN	NO	15–20 minutes
MUNG BEAN	NO	35–45 minutes
OAT GRAIN	NO	35–40 minutes
PEA — WHOLE	YES	50–60 minutes

GRAIN OR PULSE	SOAK NEEDED (if 'yes', choose *cold* or *hot* soak above)	COOKING TIME
PEA — SPLIT	NO	45–50 minutes
PINTO BEAN	YES	60–80 minutes
RED KIDNEY BEAN	YES	50–60 minutes
RICE GRAIN — LONG	NO	25–35 minutes
RICE GRAIN — SHORT	NO	20–25 minutes
RICE GRAIN — WILD	NO	45–55 minutes
RYE GRAIN	YES	50–60 minutes
SOYA BEAN	YES	2–3 hours
WHEAT GRAIN	YES	50–60 minutes

* Corn grain should be boiled in more water than usual — about 3 times rather than twice their height in water.

Sprouting Seeds

Sprouted seeds, beans and grains provide one of the most nutritionally concentrated, not to mention highly economical, sources of nourishment available. They are additive-free, pesticide-free, chemical-free, and extremely easily grown in a jar or commercially-made plastic seed-sprouter.

Alfalfa and fenugreek seeds, green lentils, mung and aduki beans, oat and wheat grains are among those which are particularly quick and easy to grow. Sprouts supply a balanced range of nutrients in an easily assimilable form, from protein and fibre to vitamins such as the B complex, A, C and E, as well as essential minerals and trace elements. They also happen to be very tasty and refreshing to eat. Use them in soups, salads, stir-fries, sandwich-fillings, and even throw a handful or two into bread recipes during the final kneading for extra taste, texture and goodness.

To grow sprouts, place two rounded tablespoons of seeds, beans and/or grains in a jar and cover them with lukewarm water. Leave to soak for 8–9 hours or overnight, then rinse thoroughly in a sieve, picking out any small twigs, grit or other foreign matter as you do so. Put them back in the jar and cover its opening with a small piece of muslin stretched over the top and kept in place with an elastic band round the neck of the jar. Pour in a little more water through the muslin, shake the jar gently with a circular motion to rinse the seeds or beans once more, then turn the jar upside-down to drain away all excess moisture (it is important to drain thoroughly, as seeds which are clogged with too much water cannot 'breathe', and will therefore decay rather than germinate). Repeat this simple rinsing and draining procedure twice a day, and the sprouts will be ready to eat after four or five days. They can be grown for up to 6–7 days, but are nutritionally at their best a day or two before this (some can also become a little tough and bitter to eat if sprouted for too long).

Store the sprouts, chilled, in a plastic container, and they will remain fresh for 3–5 days.

Gelling Agents

The most commonly used plant-based gelling agent is agar-agar, which is available in powder or flake form. This, like carrageen (another, less readily obtainable gelling agent), is derived from a type of seaweed. Agar-agar can be used for many dishes, from jellies, mousses and cold soufflés to savoury moulds (guacamole, for example, could be made with agar-agar and turned out from a mould as a shaped starter), through to the making of glazes for brushing onto fruit flans, roasts or breads and pastries. To use agar-agar, measure out two teaspoons for every pint (575ml) of liquid or creamy mixture needing to be set. Bring it to the boil with a little water, or some of the liquid being used in the recipe, and simmer it, stirring, until dissolved (2–3 minutes).

Remove from the heat and allow to cool slightly, then fold into the prepared mixture and chill to set.

Steaming Vegetables

If you have not already done so, try steaming vegetables instead of boiling them. It takes no longer than boiling, and ensures that all the nutrients remain intact. It also usually results in a better flavour and a brighter, more visually attractive vegetable, as no natural juices or colour pigment is lost in the water. Simply place the prepared vegetables in a sieve, colander or wire-mesh chip-holder (without salt — they really don't need it) and set this *above* boiling water, or anything you might have simmering on the cooker hob, such as potatoes or rice, for the usual cooking time. A bay leaf or a small pinch of rosemary added to the water beneath will ensure an agreeable cooking aroma, too!

Fine-milled Flour

It is possible to buy 100 per cent wholewheat flour which has been fine-milled, but if you cannot find any and a lighter flour is needed for baking cakes, sponges or pastries, use ordinary wholewheat flour, sift it and return the coarser bran left in the sieve to the pack of flour.

Binding Agent

For roasts, burgers and other mixtures which need some sort of binding agent to help them keep their shape, substitute one tablespoon each of soya flour and arrowroot, mixed to a thin paste with a little water, for each egg used in a conventional recipe. The soya flour/arrowroot mixture has the advantage of certain similar properties and nutritional components to those of an egg, without the latter's harmful cholesterol content.

Sugar-free Jam

This is easily made, delicious, and far more healthy in every way than the conventional highly-sugared jams and conserves. Simply place the fruit with half its weight of concentrated apple juice in a large pan, and boil them together as usual until setting point is reached. Pour into sterilized jars and cool until set. Remember to keep sugar-free jam chilled after opening, as the preserving element of sugar is, of course, absent.

Grating Fruit Rinds

I find the best way to grind orange, lemon or grapefruit rinds really finely is to peel them carefully with a potato-peeler first, leave the peeled rind on a plate for 10–15 minutes to allow some of the surface-moisture to evaporate, then grind it thoroughly in a grinder. Don't forget to wash and wipe the fruit well before using the peel, to clean it and to remove traces of chemical sprays and pesticides which may remain on it if it has not been organically grown.

Crushing Biscuit-crumbs or Nuts

Place biscuits or nuts in *two* plastic bags (commercially-made 'food-bags' will do) and, using a rolling pin for biscuits and a heavy object such as a stone, full jam-jar or small hammer for nuts, roll or pound the contents until satisfactorily crushed. This job can, of course, be done efficiently in a food-processor, if you have one.

Skinning Tomatoes

Place the tomatoes in a heatproof bowl and pour over enough freshly boiled water to cover. Leave for 30–40 seconds, then drain and peel off the skin.

Wholegrain Rice

Cook wholegrain rice in twice its volume of water (add the well-rinsed rice to the water when boiling point is reached). Simmer, covered, for 25–35 minutes until all the water has been absorbed and the rice is swollen and fluffy. In this way, where the rice is only cooked in as much water as it will absorb, no nutrients are lost in excess cooking water which then has to be thrown away.

Melba Toast

If you are not using your own baked bread for this, try making it from Vogel or another good commercially-available mixed-grain bread. It cuts quite thinly, and tastes superb!

Use of Okara

This by-product of tofu-making (see page 180) is high in fibre and contains some protein and vitamins. It can be incorporated in croquettes, rissoles and savoury roasts; dried and used to complement wholewheat flour in cakes, biscuits and crumbles (substitute okara for up to half the quantity of flour); or roasted and sprinkled over breakfast cereals or mixed with mueslis.

INDEX

Aduki beans, 184
  Aduki-coconut Salad, 122
  Golden Aduki and Millet
    Crumble, 98
  Tacos, 68
agar-agar, 31, 185
almonds:
  Almond and Cinnamon
    Filling, 175
  Almond and Mushroom
    Stroganoff, 74–5
  Aubergine and Almond
    Couscous, 85
  Cream of Melon and Almond
    Soup, 41
  Sesame-almond Cheese, 40
  Spinach and Almond
    Lasagne, 96–7
apple:
  Celery, Apple and Barley
    Soup, 43
  Spiced Apple and Banana
    Crunch, 142
apricot:
  Apricot and Almond
    Surprise, 146
  Apricot Custard Sauce, 143
  Apricot Fruit Cake, 159
aubergine:
  Aubergine and Almond
    Couscous, 85
  Aubergine and Brazil Nut
    Bake, 78
  Aubergine and Pine-Nut
    Starter, 50
  Stuffed Aubergine, 82–3
avocado:
  Avocado and Pear
    Hollandaise, 55
  Avocado, Pear and Olive
    Salad, 117

banana:
  Carrot and Banana Cake, 162

Date and Banana Ice-cream, 152
Spiced Apple and Banana
  Crunch, 142
barley:
  Celery, Apple and Barley
    Soup, 43
  Wheat and Barley Pancakes, 101
beans:
  Black-eyed Biriani, 72
  Courgette and White Bean
    Salad, 110
  Golden Aduki and Millet
    Crumble, 89
  Mixed Bean Hotpot with Sage
    Dumplings, 70–1
beetroot:
  Cooked Beetroot and Mooli
    Salad, 115
  Raw Beetroot and Carrot
    Salad, 112
binding agents, 186
biscuits see cakes and biscuits
Brazil nut:
  Aubergine and Brazil Nut
    Bake, 78
  Brazilian Brussels Sprouts, 138
breads and quickbreads, 167–78
  Cheese and Herb Scones, 177
  Fig and Ginger Bake, 173
  Malted Mixed Grain Bread, 170
  Mexican Tortillas, 178
  Quick Sunflower-seed Bread, 169
  Raisin, Bran and Wheatgerm
    Muffins, 176
  Rich Scandinavian Supper
    Ring, 174–5
  Rye-oat Bread with Caraway and
    Fennel Seeds, 171
  Sesame Corn Bread, 172
  Wheaten Soda Bread, 167
  Whole Wheat Bread, 168
broccoli:
  Broccoli and Chestnut Bake, 73
  Broccoli Tofu Soufflé, 60

Butter Spread, 30

Cakes and biscuits, 156–66
  Almond and Poppy-seed
    Cake, 156
  Aniseed and Orange
    Cookies, 166
  Apricot Fruit Cake, 159
  Blackcurrant and Hazelnut
    Slices, 164
  Carob Crumb Cake, 158
  Carob Fudge-truffles, 157
  Carrot and Banana Cake, 162
  Choc-nut Crunchies, 165
  Digestive Biscuits, 164
  Malted Carob Brownies, 163
  Orange Marzipan, 166
  Orange and Oat Cake, 162
  Peanut Butter Cookies, 164
  Peanut Health Candy, 157
  Tofu, Prune and Lemon
    Cake, 160
carob:
  Carob Crumb Cake, 158
  Carob Fudge-truffles, 157
  Carob and Orange
    Cheesecake, 150
  Malted Carob Brownies, 163
carrot:
  Carrot and Banana Cake, 161
  Carrot and Hazelnut Roast, 77
  Carrot and Peanut Soup, 45
  Ginger-glazed Carrots, 135
  Raw Beetroot and Carrot
    Salad, 112
cashew:
  Cashew Nut Cream, 33
  Cashew and Sesame Milk, 32
  Cashew and Walnut roast, 76
  Courgette and Cashew Crisp, 75
cauliflower:
  Cauliflower in Mushroom and
    Chestnut Sauce, 139

Tropical Cauliflower and Parsnip
Salad, 133
Celeriac and Sunflower Slaw, 121
celery:
Celery, Apple and Barley
Soup, 43
Celery, Cheese and Raisin
Filling, 175
cheese:
Basic Vegan Cheese, 35
Cheese and Herb Scones, 177
Cheese Sauce, 124
Cheese-nut pâté, 49
Cheesy Fennel Waldorf
Salad, 119
Chestnut Cheese, 40
Cottage Cheese, Basic, 36
Courgette, Mushroom and Cheese
Pâté, 55
Cream Cheese, 36
Curd Cheese, 37
Mixed Seed Soft Cheese, 39
Seed and Nut Soft Cheese, 39
Sesame-almond Cheese, 40
Soy-nut Cheese, 35
Tangy Spinach and Cream Cheese
Pâté, 55
Tofu and Nut Soft Cheese, 38
Tofu Ricotta, 38
Yoghurt Cheese, 36-7
Cheesecake:
Carob and Orange, 150
Maple-ginger, 149
chestnut:
Broccoli and Chestnut Bake, 73
Chestnut Cheese, 40
Chocolate-chestnut Fudge
Dessert, 152
Lentil and Chestnut Tagliatelli, 95
Chicory with Mushrooms and
Tomatoes, Braised, 141
coconut:
Aduki-coconut Salad, 122
Chilli con Coconut, 66
Coconut Cream, 34
Spiced Lentil and Coconut
Pâté, 55
Strawberry-coconut Yoghurt Ice-
cream, 153
courgette:
Almond and Tarragon Bisque, 48
Courgette and Cashew Crisp, 75
Courgette, Mushroom and Cheese
Quiche, 106-7
Courgette and White Bean
Salad, 110
Minted Courgette and Mange-
touts, 136
Stuffed Courgettes with Almond
and Rosemary Sauce, 91
Cream, 30
Cashew Nut, 33
Cheese, 36

Coconut, 34
Soured, 34
Tofu Whipped, 33
Whipped, 32
crushing, crumb or nuts, 187

dairy, vegan, 29-40
desserts *see* puddings and desserts
diet, vegan
Dressings, 123-33
Italian Garlic, 132
Lemon and Tarragon, 131
Thousand Island, 132
Tofu Mayonnaise, 133
Vinaigrette, 131

eggs, 31
equipment, 24

fennel:
Cheesy Fennel Waldorf
Salad, 119
Fennel and Mushroom Filling with
Water Chestnuts, 104
Fig and Ginger Bake, 173
Fillings, pancake:
Asparagus and Almond
Cream, 102-3
Fennel and Mushroom with Water
Chestnuts, 104
Florentine, 105
Watercress Ricotta, 106
flour, fine-milled, 186
fruit:
grating rinds, 187
Mulled Fruit Salad, 147
Three-tone Fresh Fruit Salad, 114

gelling agents, 185
grains, soaking and cooking, 182-4
Guacamole, 57

hazelnut:
Blackcurrant and Hazelnut
Slices, 164
Carrot and Hazelnut Roast, 77
Hazelnut Rice Salad, 114

Ice-cream:
Date and Banana, 152
Strawberry-Coconut Yoghurt, 153
Italian Garlic Dressing, 132

Jam, Sugar-free, 186-7
Jerusalem Artichoke Mould (Baked)
with Fines Herbes Sauce, 51

lemon:
Lemon and Tarragon
Dressing, 131
Tofu, Prune and Lemon
Cake, 160
lentil:

Lentil and Chestnut
Tagliatelle, 95
Lentil Moussaka, 69
Lentil, Walnut and Bulgar
Salad, 116
Spiced Lentil and Coconut
Pâté, 55
Spiced Spinach and Lentil
Soup, 44

margarine, 29-30
Melba Toast, 188
milk, 29
Almonds and Oatmeal, 31
Cashew and Sesame, 32
Mixed Bean Hotpot with Sage
Dumplings, 70-1
mixed grains:
Malted Mixed Grain Bread, 170
Mixed Grain Ring, 92
mushrooms:
Almond and Mushroom
Stroganoff, 74-5
Arane and Mushroom Stir-
fry, 137
Courgette, Mushroom and Cheese
Quiche, 106-7
Mushroom Cream Sauce, 125
Mushroom, Onion and Nut
Pâté, 58
Stuffed Mushrooms, 53

nuts:
Almond and Mushroom
Stroganoff, 73-4
Aubergine and Brazil Nut
Bake, 78
Brazilian Brussels Sprouts, 138
Broccoli and Chestnut Bake, 73
Carrot and Hazelnut Roast, 77
Cashew and Walnut Roast, 76
Cheese-nut Pâté, 49
Choc-nut Crunches, 165
Courgette and Cashew Nut
Crisp, 75
crushing, 187
Mushroom, Onion and Nut
Pâté, 58
Nut and Seed Croustade with
Mushroom and Tomato
Sauce, 86-7
Nutty Paella, 90
Pistachio Risotto Verde, 88
Potato-nut Salad, 118
Potato-nutmeat, 79
Quick Vegetable and Nuttolene
Fricassée, 81
Seed and Nut Soft Cheese, 39
Spinach, Peanut and Tomato
Layer, 80
Stuffed Aubergines, 82-3
Sweet and Savoury Picnic
Balls, 84

Tofu and Nut Soft Cheese, 38

oats, 184
Orange and Oak Cake, 162
Oatmeal and Almond Milk, 31, 145
okara, 180, 188
onion:
 Golden Potato and Onion
  Layer, 136
 Mushroom, Onion and Nut
  Pâté, 58
orange:
 Aniseed and Orange
  Cookies, 166
 Carob and Orange
  Cheesecake, 150
 Orange Marzipan, 166
 Orange and Oat Cake, 162
 Orange and Sesame Sautéed
  Tofu, 62
 Watercress and Orange Soup, 46

Pancakes:
 fillings see fillings, pancakes
 Wheat and Barley, 101
 Tofu, 102
parsnips:
 Sesame Baked Parsnips, 141
 Parsnip and Sesame Soup, 47
 Tropical Cauliflower and Parsnip
  Salad, 113
pasta:
 Lentil and Chestnut
  Tagliatelle, 95
 Spiced Pasta Salad, 108
 Spinach and Almond
  Lasagne, 96–7
 Tofu Pasta-noodles, 94
Pâtés, 49–58
 Cheese-nut, 49
 Mushroom, Onion and Nut, 58
 Spiced Lentil and Coconut, 55
 Tangy Spinach and Cream
  Cheese, 56
 see also starters
peanuts:
 Carrot and Peanut Soup, 45
 Peanut Butter Biscuits, 164
 Peanut Health Candy, 157
 Spinach, Peanut and Tomato
  Layer, 80
pear:
 Avocado and Pear
  Hollandaise, 55
 Avocado, Pear and Olive
  Salad, 117
Pizza:
 Pepperoni, 98–9
 Quick Unyeasted, 100–1
potato:
 Caribbean Potato Gratin, 135
 Golden Potato and Onion
  Layer, 136

Potato-nut Salad, 118
puddings and desserts, 142–55
 Apricot and Almond Surprise, 146
 Apricot Custard Sauce, 143
 Carob and Orange
  Cheescake, 150
 Chocolate-chestnut Fudge
  Dessert, 152
 Creamy Pumpkin and Pecan
  Pie, 155
 Crème Caramel, 150–1
 Date and Banana Ice-cream, 152
 Highland Ambrosia, 154
 Maple-ginger Cheesecake, 149
 Mulled Fruit Salad, 147
 Om-ali Egyptian Cracked Wheat
  Pudding, 145
 Spiced Apple and Banana
  Crunch, 142
 Strawberry-coconut Yoghurt Ice-
  cream, 153
 Strawberry and Hazelnut Cream
  Flan, 148
 Three-tone Fresh Fruit Salad, 144
pulses:
 Aduki Bean Tacos, 68
 Arabian Hummus, 71
 Black-eyed Biriani, 72
 Chilli con Coconut, 66
 Lentil Moussaka, 69
 Mixed Bean Hotpot with Sage
  Dumplings, 70–1
 soaking and cooking, 182–4

Ratatouille, 140
Red Cabbage, Prune and Pumpkin
 Slaw, 111
Rice:
 Hazelnut Rice Salad, 114
 whole grain, 187
Rye-oat Bread with Caraway and
 Fennel Seed, 171

Salads, 108–22
 Aduki-coconut, 122
 Avocado, Pear and Olive, 117
 Celeriac and Sunflower Slaw, 121
 Cheesy Fennel Waldorf, 119
 Cooked Beetroot and Mooli, 115
 Courgette and White Bean, 110
 Crisp Green and White, 120
 Hazelnut Rice, 114
 Italian Tofu and Tomato, 109
 Lentil, Walnut and Bulgar, 116
 Mulled Fruit, 147
 Potato-nut, 118
 Raw Beetroot and Carrot, 112
 Red Cabbage, Prune and Pumpkin
  Slaw, 111
 Spiced Pasta Salad, 108
 Three-tone Fresh Fruit, 144
 Tropical Cauliflower and
  Parsnip, 113

Sauces, 123–33
 Almond and Rosemary, 127
 Apricot Custard, 143
 Barbecue, 129
 Cheese, 124
 Curry, 128
 Fine Herbes, 124
 Hollandaise, 130
 Mushroom Cream, 125
 Savoury Brown, 126
 Tartare, 130
 Tomato, 127
seeds and grains:
 Aubergine and Almond
  Couscous, 85
 Almond and Poppy-seed
  Cake, 156
 Golden Aduki and Millet
  Crumble, 89
 Mixed Grain Ring, 92
 Mixed Seed Soft Cheese, 39
 Nut and Seed Croustade with
  Mushroom and Tomato
  Sauce, 86–7
 Nutty Paella, 90
 Pistachio Risotto Verde, 88
 sprouting seeds, 184–5
 Stuffed Courgettes with Almond
  and Rosemary Sauce, 91
 Tomato-baked Nori Roulade, 93
Sesame:
 Cashew and Sesame Milk, 40
 Orange and Sesame Sautéed
  Tofu, 62
 Parsnip and Sesame Soup, 47
 Sesame-almond Cheese, 40
 Sesame Baked Parsnips, 141
 Sesame Corn Bread, 172
shortenings, 29–30
soaking, pulses and grains, 182–3
soups, 41–8
 Carrot and Peanut, 45
 Celery, Apple and Barley, 43
 Cream of Melon and Almond, 41
 Spiced Spinach and Lentil, 44
 Tomato and Dill, 42
 Vegetable Stock, 41
 Watercress and Orange, 46
soured cream, 34
spice:
 Apple and Banana Crunch, 142
 Lentil and Coconut Pâté, 55
 Pasta Salad, 108
 Red Cabbage with Apple, 138
spinach:
 Spiced Spinach and Lentil
  Soup, 44
 Spinach and Almond
  Lasagne, 96–7
 Spinach, Peanut and Tomato
  Layer, 80
 Tangy Spinach and Cream Cheese
  Pâté, 56

spreads, butter, 30
sprouting seeds, 184–5
Sprouts, Brazilian Brussels, 138
starters, 49–58
  Aubergine and Pine-nut, 50
  Avocado and Pear
    Hollandaise, 55
  Baked Jerusalem Artichoke
    Mould, 51
  Crispy Tofu Crunches with Tartare
    Sauce, 52
  Guacamole, 57
  Stuffed Mushrooms, 53
  Tofu in Watercress
    Mayonnaise, 54
  see also pâtés
steaming vegetables, 186
stock, vegetable, 41
strawberry:
  Strawberry-coconut Yoghurt Ice-
    cream, 153
  Strawberry and Hazelnut-cream
    Flan, 148
Stuffed:
  Aubergines, 82–3
  Mushrooms, 53
Sunflower seed:
  Bread, Quick, 169
  Celeriac and Sunflower
    Salad, 121
Swiss Chard with Chestnuts, 137

tofu:
  Barbecued Tofu, 59
  Broccoli Tofu Soufflé, 60
  Crispy Tofu Crunches with Tartare
    Sauce, 52

instructions for making, 179–81
Javanese Sunflower Tofu, 64
Orange and Sesame Sautéed
  Tofu, 64
Savory Tofu Loaf, 63
Singapore Kebabs, 61
Tofu Foo Yong, 65
Tofu Mayonnaise, 133
Tofu and Nut Soft Cheese, 38
Tofu Pasta-noodles, 94
Tofu Pancakes, 102
Tofu Prune and Lemon
  Cake, 160
Tofu Ricotta Cheese, 38
Tofu in Watercress
  Mayonnaise, 54
Tofu in Whipped Cream, 33
tomato:
  Italian Tofu and Tomato
    Sauce, 109
  skinning tomatoes, 187
  Tomato Baked Nori Roulade, 93
  Tomato and Dill Soup, 42
  Tomato Sauce, 127
Tortillas, Mexican, 178

Vegan Cheese, Basic, 35
veganism, 8–28
vegetables:
  Arame and Mushroom Stir-
    fry, 137
  Braised Chicory with Mushrooms
    and Tomatoes, 141
  Brazilian Brussels Sprouts, 138
  Caribbean Potato Gratin, 135
  Cauliflower in Mushroom and
    Chestnut Sauce, 139

Ginger-glazed Carrots, 135
Golden Potato and Onion
  Layer, 136
Minted Courgettes and Mange-
  touts, 136
Quick Vegetable and Nuttolene
  Fricassée, 81
Ratatouille, 140
Sesame Baked Parsnips, 141
Spiced Red Cabbage with
  Apple, 138
steaming, 186
Swiss Chard with Water
  Chestnuts, 137
Vegetable Mélange, 134
Vegetable stock, 41
vitamins, 14–15, 23, 184

walnuts:
  Cashew and Walnut Roast, 76
  Lentil, Walnut and Bulgar
    Salad, 116
watercress:
  Watercress and Orange Soup, 46
  Watercress and Ricotta
    Filling, 106
wheat:
  grains, 184
  Lentil, Walnut and Bulgar
    Salad, 116
  Om-ali Egyptian Cracked-wheat
    pudding, 145
  Wheat and Barley Pancakes, 101
Whipped cream, 32
  Tofu, 33

yoghurt, 30–1
  cheese, 36–7